EAT
ME!

Dearest Mummy Goose, this book is for you.
For your unfailing belief in me, the clothes you
have made me, the stories you have read me, and
for teaching me to bake in the first place.

EAT ME!

The Stupendous, Self-Raising World
of Cupcakes & Bakes According to

Cookie Girl

EBURY
PRESS

3 5 7 9 10 8 6 4

Published in 2010 by Ebury Press, an imprint of Ebury Publishing
Ebury Publishing is a division of the Random House Group

Text © Xanthe Milton 2010
Photography by Simon Brown 2010

The Random House Group Limited Reg. No. 954009

Addresses for companies within the Random House Group
can be found at www.randomhouse.co.uk

A CIP catalogue record for this book is available from the British Library

The Random House Group makes every effort to ensure that the
papers used in our books are made from trees that have been legally
sourced from well-managed and credibly certified forests. Our
paper procurement policy can be found on www.randomhouse.co.uk

Design: Georgia Vaux
Illustrations: Louise Scott-Smith
Copy editor: Jinny Johnson
Photographer: Simon Brown
Stylist: Tessa Evelegh
Food stylist: Nancy Campbell

The publishers would like to thank Jane Sacchi for lending her
exquisite French bedlinen: antique monogrammed sheet and pillowcases
and antique indigo-dyed French hemp sheet all from Jane Sacchi
(tel: 020 7351 3160,www.janesacchi.squarespace.com). Also thanks to
From Somewhere for the author's shirt (page 160) and to Let Them Eat Cake
(www.letthemeatcake.bigcartel.com) for the cake stands.

Printed and bound in Italy by Graphicom

ISBN: 9780091925116

To buy books by your favourite authors and
register for offers visit www.rbooks.co.uk

Contents

Introduction

There is a myth that surrounds baking – a kind of mystique that puts many people off for no good reason. This is a pity, as few things in life give you as much satisfaction for so little effort. There is something so joyful about taking a batch of cupcakes from the oven, and smelling their warm, heady aroma. I have yet to meet anyone, young or old, man or woman, who does not get a kick out of this. It is ridiculously pleasing to see how a batter prepared from everyday ingredients rises to such exemplary proportions, bringing gasps of admiration from all who see the results.

There is an important thing to remember when baking: you must believe in it. It may sound strange, but I think that cookies and cakes can sense when you are full of doubt, and that is when they sink in the middle, spill over the edges or just taste plain wrong. Baking is a form of alchemy and, as with magic, you have to believe in it for it to work.

So when making cupcakes for a wedding, it is essential to think thoughts of love, future happiness and prosperity for the bride and groom. Visualise their many happy years together as you stir the mixture. When baking cakes for birthday boys and girls, imagine wonderful wishes coming true. Take an arrow from Cupid's quiver and aim it at a heart-shaped biscuit for your Valentine.

Never bake out of a sense of obligation or when feeling sad or stressed. No good will come of it – the milk will sour and the butter will go rancid. Take a moment to think about how you want the cake or biscuit to taste, have a cup of tea and shake off your troubles. Smile and remind yourself that you are not going to let anything cloud your ability to make something tremendous and life-enhancing.

Food has the power to take us on an incredible journey. We can revisit those lost years of childhood with just one mouthful of a cake or biscuit like granny used to bake. There is nothing quite like a freshly baked cookie or cupcake to bring a sense of comfort, belonging and completeness. Here are some of my cake memories: curled up like a kitten on Grandma's worn Damask sofa, nibbling a lemon finger; slathering green icing onto a simple vanilla sponge to create froggy cakes for Halloween; my sister surprising me with the gift of a beautiful glass jar filled with hand-made macaroons.

These are my memories, moments that I can capture in a cupcake case, and I love passing my traditions on to the next generation. But these are just my experiences, my creations. It is up to you to make your own voyage of discovery, unleash your deepest thoughts and fancies, and create unique and satisfying ideas to pass down to your children.

Don't feel obliged to follow a recipe too rigidly – it is just a guide and an expression of my own ideas. Don't let a missing ingredient put you off – improvise and discover a whole new territory. Let seasons and occasions inspire you, be guided by the likes and dislikes of your friends and family, take risks with combinations. And if things go wrong, don't feel too bad – what is life without taking risks? The cost of the ingredients is negligible; just make sure you have enough left to create the next masterpiece.

When it comes to decorating, there are no rules. I love to use myriad sprinkles in every hue, some that catch the light like delicate jewels: gold and silver hearts and stars, colourful dragées and iridescent glitter. Flowers come in all shapes and sizes, from romantic roses in blushing pink to elegant lilies, brazen daisies and multicoloured pansies. There are Smarties, perfect for creating eyes, ears and noses for a whole menagerie of animals, and long threads of liquorice that can be wound into shapes. Sometimes just one chocolate-covered coffee bean is enough to finish off an elegant, white-iced espresso cupcake. At other times, cakes cry out to be drenched in a mountain of pick and mix, all jostling for space.

Before we start, I must warn you that baking is addictive. It's not only the eating of the cakes, but also the tremendous joy that comes with the making of them. Baking gives you the opportunity to express your creative side, from the choice of flavour to how elaborately you choose to decorate your little works of art. You will become hooked and so will all your friends and family, for there is no sweeter gift you can give.

Baking Basics

Before you get started, here are some guidelines on the equipment you'll need – nothing fancy – and a few other tips.

Equipment

Measuring scales. I use an ancient Salter scale, but any kind is fine, as long as it does the job. Once you become more experienced you can improvise if scales aren't available. A heaped tablespoon of dry ingredients is roughly 30 g/1 oz. Always weigh ingredients in either metric or imperial – don't mix the two.

Measuring jug. This can be metal, glass, china or plastic and should have measurements marked in fluid ounces and millilitres. It is easiest to be accurate with your measurements if you can see through the jug – bend down to get your eye in line with the top of the fluid.

Measuring spoons. For accuracy, it is best to have a set of measuring spoons and they don't cost much. If you have to use ordinary spoons, 1 dessertspoon is equivalent to 2 teaspoons.

Mixing bowls. I like Pyrex as it can be used in the microwave, freezer and oven. You will need a bowl large enough to contain all ingredients for a batch of cupcakes and still have room to give them a thorough mix without any spillage – about 6–8 litres is ideal. A medium, 4-litre bowl is useful for whisking egg whites, making icing, or a smaller quantity of mixture. Finally, you need at least one small bowl for softening butter in the microwave and a multitude of other uses.

Wooden spoons. Good to have a selection of these. The larger the amount you are mixing, the longer the handle you need.

Hand whisk. Useful for getting rid of lumps that the wooden spoon misses and for whisking cream or egg whites — bear in mind this takes a firm hand and a lot of patience.

Electric whisk. Not essential but makes much of the baking process a lot quicker. I couldn't do without one of these for whisking egg whites and double cream. For creaming butter and sugar, an electric whisk is the most efficient tool. You can also use a hand whisk or a wooden spoon, but it will take you longer.

Spatula. We used to call this a child cheater because it got almost every last spot of mixture out of the bowl, leaving only a measly offering for desperate little ones. It's worth spending more to get something properly flexible. Mini-spatulas are useful for getting the last drop of something out of a jar or other narrow container.

Muffin tin. This should be made of non-stick metal or silicon and be quite deep. All my recipes for cupcakes are designed to fill a 12-hole muffin tin — it really is worth investing in a proper muffin tin as fairy cake tins won't do the job as well.

Baking sheet. I use heavy enamel sheets that are quite shallow and fit into the oven without needing a shelf.

Baking tin. You will need one of these for shortbread, tray bakes and gingerbread.

Paper cases. Any paper cases will do as long as they fit the tin. See the list of suppliers on page 160 for a wide variety of attractive decorated cases. You can also get flexible cupcake baking trays that do not require cases.

Baking parchment. Use non-stick baking parchment to line baking sheets and large cake tins. A blob of soft butter on the underside of the parchment will secure the paper to the tin.

Palette knife. This is like a wide blunt knife with no cutting edge and is useful for spreading icing on top of cakes.

Icing nozzles and piping bag. Try a selection of nozzles to see what effects you can create. It is usual to work around the cake in a circular pattern, starting at the outside and working in, then finishing with a peak. You can also create a beautiful rose effect by working from the inside out. Be patient and let cakes get completely cold before icing.

Microwave. This does have a very useful role to play in baking – if you haven't remembered to leave the butter to come to room temperature you can pop it in the microwave for 10–30 seconds to soften it up.

Oven gloves and tea towels. Make sure you have plenty of these – I cannot count the number of times I have burnt myself!

Ingredients

Butter. Always use unsalted butter at room temperature, unless otherwise specified. The butter should be soft but not melted.

Eggs. Eggs should be large unless otherwise specified, preferably free-range or organic, and at room temperature if possible.

Food colouring. I always use food colouring paste not liquid, which can disrupt the balance of the recipe.

Sugar. Use caster sugar unless otherwise specified. Light brown and dark brown sugar is not the same as muscovado sugar, which gives a much darker, toffee-like result.

Storage. Most of my cakes are best eaten the day they are made, but you can freeze them before decorating. If, for some unimaginable reason, you do have cakes left at the end of the day, store them in an airtight tin.

Note on Recipes

The number of cakes each recipe yields should be viewed as a general guideline only – you may find you have enough mixture for a few more, in which case replenish your tin after the first batch has cooked. Complete cupcake novices may want to start with the basic Vanilla cupcakes on page 135 and progress from there.

Spring

Once upon a time, there
were luscious limes and lemons...

Spring is here and the earth is being nudged awake by the first sprightly flowers. Snowdrops nuzzle their way out of the dark, dank soil, proving they are not as fragile as they look. Next come curd-yellow daffodils, shaking us out of the seemingly never-ending winter gloom. Close behind them are delicate narcissi and boldly coloured primroses, which gladden our hearts with every glance.

I look out at the scene unfolding before me as my garden comes to life. Birds are flying back from their winter homes and squirrels play kiss-chase along my garden wall. In the fields, cotton-wool lambs frisk and baby cows amble behind their mothers, so it seems appropriate that we should be celebrating our own mothers at this time of year.

I remember spring days when Mum and I would amble around the antique shops in our local town. Often a sudden downpour would force us to seek shelter amid the heavy beams and sloping floors of our favourite tea shop. Here we would drink tea, chat and giggle, but most of all we would eat cake. Mum usually chose something with fruit or almonds. My choice was always the same: a large slice of coffee and walnut cake, moist, tender sponge the colour of a conker and filled with a tooth-achingly sweet butter icing. Every time, Mum would have a taste and utter the inevitable: 'Oh, I do love a slice of coffee cake!' It remains a mystery to me why she never ordered one!

One Mother's Day, when I was very young, I found a cake in a book that I so wanted to make for my mother, a cake with beautiful pale roses and sprays of yellow blossom resting elegantly on an iced basket base. In those days it was tricky to get the paste for modelling the flowers, so my big sister suggested that we fashion them from tin foil. The result was not what I had planned, so the following year I spent weeks tracking down what I needed. I was thrilled with the result, although looking at the photo now it must be said that my flowers were a little more garish than those in the book.

On a more recent Mother's Day I decided to bake Mum a cake with all the flavours she loves best in imaginative new combinations. I created a moist lemony sponge, using tart yoghurt instead of butter, and drizzled a simple glaze of fragrant elderflower over the top. The heady floral scent took me back to my childhood when I used to help her pick the elderflowers for her wine and my lemonade – on more than one occasion the precious wine was drunk by my naughty brother and his friends.

Easter is an opportunity for all my family to celebrate together. Every year for as long as I can remember we have decamped to a house called Shimpling Place for Easter. This is a wonderful, rambling Tudor mansion, with sloping floors and crumbling walls. Every inch of every wall is covered in paintings and fabric, and a rich tapestry of many lives documented in sepia-toned photographs. As a child, I couldn't figure out how the layout worked. It was as if warren after warren stretched ahead and each room seemed as if it could take you to Wonderland. I felt like Alice as I skipped along, thinking that that behind any of these doors could be a Cheshire cat or Tweedledum and Tweedledee. Even now the house has a fairy-tale hold over me. I feel as if anything is possible when I sit writing by a blazing fire, with those solid 700-year-old walls protecting me. Everywhere you look there are paintings and evocations of artistry and fantasy. It is a place where the imagination runs wild, dreams become reality and nothing is beyond your reach.

Easter is the second most important event in our family calendar and it revolves around an egg hunt in the grounds of the house. Each of us (adults included) is given a different coloured ribbon that matches the basket we must hunt for. If you see a basket that does not have your ribbon you must leave it be, unless it belongs to a particularly small member of the search party, in which case you might point them in the right direction. When I find my own basket, perhaps half hidden by a mulberry bush, it is overflowing with Easter eggs and tiny, fluffy yellow chicks, which reappear, as if by magic, year after year.

I spend the day immersed in activities with the children. The table gradually fills with seasonal delicacies. Pastel-hued eggs rest in shimmering swirls of chocolate butter icing, forming edible nests. A delicious combination of almonds and raspberries in a dense cake makes a refreshing change from all the chocolate, as does a delicately flavoured biscuit sandwich with a passion fruit filling. At the end of the weekend I take all the leftover chocolate eggs and use up the odds and ends to make magnificently decadent chocolate cookies. Batches are wrapped in pastel-coloured paper and tied with string for everyone to enjoy on their journey home.

Lemon and elderflower cupcakes

W ho would ever guess that these luscious, lemony delights are made without any butter? Their moist, yielding texture makes for a real treat, and replacing the butter with low-fat Greek yoghurt means they are almost guilt free – so why not have another? If you cannot find low-fat Greek yoghurt (I get mine at the supermarket), use any other natural yoghurt. *Makes 12.*

200 g/7 oz plain flour
2 tsp baking powder
225 g/8 oz granulated sugar
45 g/1½ oz ground almonds
finely grated zest of
    1 unwaxed lemon
2 large eggs
90 ml/3 fl oz sunflower oil

250 ml/8½ fl oz low-
    fat Greek yoghurt
½ tbsp lemon essence

For the icing
225 g/8 oz icing sugar
1 tsp elderflower cordial
4 tsp water

1. Preheat the oven to 180°C/ 350°F/Gas 4. Line a 12-hole non-stick muffin tin with paper muffin cases.

2. Sift the flour and baking powder into a large bowl. Sprinkle over the sugar and ground almonds, followed by the grated lemon zest, and mix everything together.

3. In a separate bowl, lightly beat the eggs with the oil and Greek yoghurt. Add the lemon essence.

4. Slowly pour the wet ingredients into the dry and stir with a wooden spoon. Mix until everything is combined and there are no clumps of dry ingredients.

5. Spoon the mixture into the paper cases so that they are three-quarters full. Bake the cakes in the centre of the preheated oven for about 20 minutes until they are firm and springy to the touch. Remove from the oven and place the cakes on a wire rack to cool.

6. To make the icing, sift the icing sugar into a medium-sized bowl. Add the elderflower cordial and water a little at a time to achieve a thick, creamy consistency.

7. When the cakes are cool, spoon a tablespoon of icing onto each one. Serve plain or decorate with little sugar flowers or thin shavings of lemon rind.

Hummingbird cupcakes

These yummy cakes are full of tropical flavours, hence their exotic name. I like to add colourful decorations. *Makes 12.*

110 g/4 oz plain flour
½ tsp baking powder
¼ tsp bicarbonate of soda
¼ tsp salt
1 large egg
1 large egg yolk
225 g/8 oz golden caster sugar
120 ml/4 fl oz sunflower oil
1 tsp vanilla extract
120 ml/4 fl oz soured cream
1 tsp cinnamon
1 banana, mashed
55 g/2 oz pecans, chopped
150 ml/5 fl oz canned crushed
    pineapple, drained

For the icing
85 g/3 oz unsalted butter,
    room temperature
85 g/3 oz cream cheese,
    room temperature
450 g/1 lb icing sugar, sifted
peach food colouring paste
    (optional)
white chocolate buttons with
    hundreds and thousands,
    to decorate

1. Preheat the oven to 180°C/ 350°F/Gas 4. Line a 12-hole non-stick muffin tin with paper cases.

2. Sift the flour, baking powder, bicarbonate and salt into a bowl.

3. In a separate bowl, whisk together the egg, egg yolk and sugar until the mixture becomes pale and slightly thickens. Continue whisking as you add the oil and vanilla.

4. Stir in the soured cream until it is incorporated, then add the flour mixture followed by the cinnamon, banana, pecans and pineapple. If you can't find canned crushed pineapple, buy a can of pineapple, drain and crush it with a wooden spoon.

5. Spoon the mixture into the paper cases so that they are three-quarters full. Bake the cakes in the centre of the preheated oven for about 20 minutes. Check with a skewer – if the cakes are cooked the skewer should come out clean. Remove from the oven and place the cakes on a wire rack to cool.

6. Meanwhile, make the icing. Using an electric whisk, mix the butter and cream cheese. Add the icing sugar a third at a time, beating thoroughly after each addition. Add a dot or two of peach food colouring, if you like.

7. Ice the cakes when they are cool, using a piping bag fitted with a plain nozzle. Decorate with the chocolate buttons and add some extra icing in different colours if you feel adventurous.

French toast cupcakes

When I first invented these cakes my family simply couldn't get enough of them. They really do taste like the French toast they are named after. I think they look cute with light brown icing and miniature gingerbread men sprinkled on top (see Suppliers, page 160). *Makes 12.*

170 g/6 oz plain flour
1½ tsp baking powder
½ tsp ground cinnamon
¼ tsp salt
110 g/4 oz unsalted butter
225 g/8 oz granulated sugar
2 large eggs
2 tsp vanilla extract
2 tsp maple syrup
50 ml/2 fl oz milk

For the icing
110 g/4 oz unsalted butter,
    room temperature
110 g/4 oz cream cheese,
    room temperature
450 g/1 lb icing sugar, sifted
¼ tsp cinnamon
brown food colouring paste
    (optional)
sprinkles, to decorate

1. Preheat the oven to 180°C/350°F/Gas 4. Line a 12-hole non-stick muffin tin with paper cases.

2. Sift the flour, baking powder, cinnamon and salt into a bowl. Melt the butter and let it cool slightly.

3. In a large bowl, whisk the sugar and eggs together, then add the melted butter. Mix the vanilla, maple syrup and milk in a separate bowl.

4. Now stir the flour mixture into the sugar, eggs and butter, followed by the milk mixture. Beat until everything is well combined.

5. Divide the mixture between the paper cases (each should be three-quarters full). Bake in the centre of the preheated oven for 20 minutes. A skewer inserted should come out clean if the cakes are cooked. Remove the cakes from the oven and place on a wire rack to cool.

6. Meanwhile, make the icing. Using an electric whisk, mix the butter and cream cheese. Add the icing sugar, a third at a time, beating thoroughly after each addition. Add the cinnamon with the last of the icing sugar. Add a dot or two of food colouring, if you like.

7. Using a piping bag with a straight-edged nozzle, pipe icing onto the cakes, working from the outside into a peak in the centre. Decorate with sprinkles – I like to use gingerbread men.

Black Forest cupcakes

When I was a child, Black Forest gateau was just about the biggest treat I could imagine. It was also one of my mum's favourites, so I took great delight in reconstructing the recipe as a cupcake for her and presenting them in a box for Mother's Day. She protested, saying, 'Oh you are naughty. I really shouldn't.' But her cries of protest were muffled by mouthfuls of cake! *Makes 9.*

110 g/4 oz unsalted butter,
    room temperature
110 g/4 oz golden caster sugar
2 eggs
½ tbsp golden syrup
110 g/4 oz self-raising flour
1 tsp baking powder
2 tbsp cocoa powder

For the cherry filling
110 g/4 oz black cherry jam
½ tbsp kirsch

For the topping
1 small can of black cherries
100 ml/3½ fl oz double cream
1 tbsp grated plain chocolate

1. Preheat the oven to 170°C/325°F/Gas 3. Take a 12-hole non-stick muffin tin and line nine of the holes with paper muffin cases.

2. Cream the butter and sugar together until pale and fluffy. Add the eggs, one at a time, beating well after each addition. Add the golden syrup. Sift the flour, baking powder and cocoa powder together into a bowl and gently fold into the batter.

3. Divide the mixture between the paper cases. Bake the cakes in the centre of the oven for 20 minutes until the tops are springy to the touch. Remove from the oven and place the cakes on a wire rack to cool.

4. To make the cherry filling, blend the jam and kirsch together. Set aside half for spreading on the cakes.

5. Once the cakes are cool, remove the centre of each one with a sharp knife or an apple corer. Half-fill the hole with cherry filling, then pop a cherry on top. When all of the cakes have been filled in this way, spread some of the reserved cherry filling on top of each one, using the back of a spoon or a palette knife.

6. Whip the cream until it forms soft peaks. Using a piping bag with a star nozzle, pipe some cream onto each cake. Add a cherry on top, if you like, and sprinkle with a little grated chocolate.

Hazelnut marble cupcakes

When my niece made this cake I was about to set off on a long journey and was feeling rather below par, so I wasn't sure I wanted any. She insisted it would do me good and wrapped a large slab in foil. On the way home I began nibbling on it and the more I ate the better I felt. By the time I got home I had never felt better. Perhaps it's just me, but I think this recipe has almost magical properties, so here it is in cupcake form. *Makes 12.*

110 g/4 oz hazelnuts, roughly chopped
110 g/4 oz plain chocolate, chopped
110 g/4 oz unsalted butter
140 g/5 oz golden caster sugar
2 large eggs
75 ml/2½ fl oz milk
200 g/7 oz self-raising flour
1 tsp baking powder
30 g/1 oz plain chocolate chips
1 tsp vanilla extract
icing sugar, to decorate

1. Preheat the oven to 170°C/ 325°F/Gas 3. Line a 12-hole non-stick muffin tin with paper muffin cases.

2. Once the oven is hot, place the hazelnuts on a baking sheet and roast for 6–8 minutes. Keep a close eye on them and don't let them burn. Allow the nuts to cool, and then chop them roughly to the size of about a quarter of a nut.

3. Melt the plain chocolate in a bowl over a pan of simmering water or in a microwave. Allow to cool.

4. Cream the butter and sugar together until light and fluffy. Add the eggs, one at a time, followed by the milk.

5. Sift the flour and baking powder together and gently fold into the mixture.

6. Divide the mixture in half. Add the melted chocolate and chocolate chips to one bowl and the vanilla and hazelnuts to the other.

7. Spoon the mixture into the cases, alternating teaspoons of the two flavours until the case is almost full. Bake the cakes in the centre of the preheated oven for about 20 minutes until they are firm and springy to the touch. Remove from the oven and place the cakes on a wire rack to cool.

8. Sprinkle with icing sugar to decorate.

Coffee walnut cupcakes

These have a deliciously strong coffee flavour and are packed full of walnuts, just how my mum loves them. If they are to be enjoyed by children you might prefer to use half the amount of coffee. *Makes 12.*

110 g/4 oz unsalted butter,
    room temperature
110 g/4 oz sugar
2 large eggs
110 g/4 oz self-raising flour
1 tsp baking powder
1 tbsp instant coffee dissolved
    in 1 tbsp of boiling water
55 g/2 oz walnuts, chopped

For the filling
55 g/2 oz unsalted butter,
    room temperature

110 g/4 oz icing sugar, sifted
1 tbsp instant coffee dissolved
    in 1 tbsp of boiling water

For the icing
1 tbsp instant coffee dissolved
    in 1 tbsp of boiling water
140 g/5 oz icing sugar, sifted

For decoration
12 walnut halves

1. Preheat the oven to 180°C/ 350°F/Gas 4. Line a 12-hole non-stick muffin tin with paper cases.

2. Cream the butter and sugar together until pale and fluffy, then beat in the eggs one at a time. Sift the flour and baking powder together and add this, a third at a time, to the batter. Follow with the coffee mixture and the nuts.

3. Spoon the mixture into the paper cases so that they are three-quarters full. Bake in the centre of the oven for about 20 minutes until they are firm and springy to the touch. Remove from the oven and place the cakes on a wire rack to cool.

4. To make the filling, cream the butter and sugar together and add the coffee mixture. When the cakes are cool, remove a small section from the centre of each one with a sharp knife or an apple corer. Spoon in the filling, pushing it down so that the cake is well filled.

5. To make the icing, add the coffee water to the icing sugar a teaspoon at a time until you get a mixture the consistency of double cream. You should be able to spread the icing over the top of each cake without it dripping off. If the icing seems too thin, add a little more icing sugar to thicken it. Decorate the top of each cake with a walnut half.

Carrot cookie creams

Any cookie that contains a vegetable leads me to believe that it can only be a good thing to make – and eat – as many as possible. The fact that these cookies contain the goodness of the humble oat, too, must mean that they are doubly good for me – double helpings, surely? *Makes about 30 (15 sandwiches).*

185 g/3 oz unsalted butter,
    room temperature
200 g/7 oz plain flour, sifted
170 g/6 oz soft brown sugar
85 g/3 oz granulated sugar
1 egg
1 tsp baking powder
½ tsp cinnamon
¼ tsp bicarbonate of soda
¼ tsp ground cloves
½ tsp vanilla extract

110 g/4 oz oatmeal
2 medium carrots, grated
55 g/2 oz raisins (optional)

For the icing
110 g/4 oz cream cheese,
    room temperature
200 g/7 oz icing sugar, sifted
55 g/2 oz unsalted butter,
    room temperature
1 tbsp fresh lemon juice

1. Preheat the oven to 170°C/ 325°F/Gas 3. You will need a large ungreased baking sheet.

2. Place the butter in a mixing bowl and beat by hand for 2 minutes until softened.

3. Add half the flour, both sugars, egg, baking powder, cinnamon, bicarbonate, cloves and vanilla. Beat until everything is combined, scraping the sides of the bowl occasionally to bring in all the ingredients. Mix in the remaining flour and stir in the oatmeal, carrots and raisins, if using.

4. Drop rounded teaspoons of dough onto the baking sheet, leaving 5cm/2in between each one.

5. Bake in the preheated oven for 10–12 minutes or until the edges of the cookies are golden. Remove from the oven and leave the cookies to cool on the baking sheet for 10 minutes before transferring them to a wire rack to cool.

6. For the icing, beat the cream cheese with the icing sugar. Add the butter followed by the lemon juice and continue to beat until the icing has a smooth, creamy consistency.

7. Using a spatula, spread a spoonful of soft-cheese icing on the flat side of a cookie. Top with another cookie, flat-side down, to make a cookie sandwich. Repeat with the rest of the cookies.

Lemon finger cookies

These delicate biscuits are just divine. The usually rich buttercream filling is cut through with the tart zing of lemon, so the cookies taste dangerously light and are impossible to resist. *Makes about 8 filled cookie sandwiches.*

225 g/8 oz unsalted butter,
    room temperature
55 g/2 oz icing sugar
½ tsp vanilla essence
grated zest of 3 lemons
225 g/8 oz plain flour
3 tbsp cornflour

For the filling
55 g/2 oz unsalted butter,
    room temperature
125 g/4½ oz icing sugar
zest of 2 lemons
juice of ½ lemon

1. Preheat the oven to 170°C/ 325°F/Gas 3. You will need a large ungreased baking sheet.

2. Beat the butter with the icing sugar, vanilla and lemon zest until light and fluffy.

3. Sift the flour and cornflour together and stir into the creamed mixture.

4. Using a 1.2cm/½in fluted nozzle and piping bag, pipe fingers of the mixture onto a baking sheet. You should have about 16 fingers, 5cm/2in long. Leave 2.5cm/1in between each one.

5. Bake the cookies in the preheated oven for 12 minutes. Remove from the oven and leave them to firm up on the baking sheet before transferring to a wire rack to cool.

6. To make the filling, beat the butter with the icing sugar, lemon zest and juice until light and fluffy.

7. Spread the filling onto the flat side of half the cookies. Top with the remaining cookies to make cookie sandwiches. Unfilled cookies keep for five days; filled cookies for three days.

Passion fruit sandwiches

In this recipe, delicious shimmering passion fruit curd is held together by fragile buttery thins. The curd tends to ooze out as you eat, so a plate is essential and perhaps a surreptitious stroke with your finger – the filling is way too good to waste. *Makes 12–15 filled sandwiches.*

125 g/4½ oz unsalted butter,
   room temperature
125 g/4½ oz caster sugar
½ tsp vanilla extract
3 egg whites
125 g/4½ oz plain flour

For the curd filling
10 passion fruit
85 g/3 oz unsalted butter
2 large eggs
2 large egg yolks
110 g/4 oz caster sugar
2 tbsp cornflour

1. Preheat the oven to 190°C/ 375°F/Gas 5. Line a baking sheet with greaseproof paper.

2. In a large bowl, cream the butter and sugar together until light and fluffy. Add the vanilla and mix well.

3. Whisk the egg whites in a separate bowl until they form stiff peaks. Using a metal spoon, very gently fold the egg whites into the butter and sugar mixture. Sift the flour on top of the mixture and fold it in very gently.

4. Using a piping bag with a medium-sized plain nozzle, pipe 7.5cm/3in fingers of the mixture onto the baking sheet (with 2.5cm/ 1in gaps between to allow for spreading). Bake for 6–8 minutes until crispy and pale gold at the edges. Cool on a wire rack.

5. Now make the curd filling. Cut the passion fruits in half and strain

the juice into a bowl. Set aside the seeds and pulp. Heat the butter and strained fruit juice in a pan over a medium heat until the butter melts.

6. In a bowl, whisk the eggs, egg yolks and sugar together until blended. Dissolve the cornflour in 4 tablespoons of cold water and whisk into the egg mixture. Continue whisking as you slowly add the hot butter and passion fruit juice.

7. Pour everything back into the pan. Cook over a medium heat, stirring with a wooden spoon, until the curd comes to the boil and thickens (about 5 minutes). Remove from the heat and add the reserved seeds and pulp. Leave to cool.

8. Spoon the curd into a piping bag with a medium-sized plain nozzle. Pipe curd onto the flat side of half the biscuits. Place another biscuit on top to create sandwiches.

Easter nest cupcakes

These are incredibly rich and fantastically chocolatey. You must use a piping bag to ice them so that you can create the rough look of a bird's nest. I like to scatter sugar flowers on the edges before filling the nests with sugar-coated chocolate eggs. *Makes 12.*

55 g/2 oz cocoa powder
240 ml/8 fl oz boiling water
200 g/7 oz plain flour
2 tsp baking powder
150 g/5 oz unsalted butter,
   room temperature
200 g/7 oz granulated sugar
2 large eggs
2 tsp vanilla extract

For the icing
85 g/3 oz plain chocolate
285 g/10 oz icing sugar
1½ tbsp cocoa powder
340 g/12 oz unsalted butter,
   room temperature
1 tsp vanilla extract
120 ml/4 fl oz double cream
coloured chocolate mini eggs,
   to decorate

1. Preheat the oven to 180°C/ 350°F/Gas 4. Line a 12-hole non-stick muffin tin with paper cases.

2. Blend the cocoa powder and boiling water together until smooth. Leave to cool to room temperature. Sift together the flour and baking powder and set aside.

3. Cream the butter and sugar together until pale and fluffy. Add the eggs and vanilla, stir well and add the sifted flour and baking powder. Mix again until smooth, then add the cooled chocolate mixture and beat again.

4. Divide the mixture between the paper cases. Bake in the centre of the preheated oven for about 20 minutes until the cakes feel light and springy to the touch. Remove from the oven and place on a wire rack to cool.

5. Next, make the icing. Melt the chocolate in a bowl over a pan of simmering water. Allow to cool slightly. Sift the icing sugar and cocoa powder into a large bowl. Add the butter and beat until blended.

6. Whisk the melted chocolate, vanilla and cream into the icing-sugar mixture. Beat for about 3 minutes until it is smooth and creamy and the colour begins to lighten. Cool briefly. Spoon the icing into a piping bag with a star nozzle and pipe onto the cakes to give the effect of a nest. Top each one with 4 or 5 mini eggs.

Easter cookies

S ometimes (very rarely in my family) you need something plain, simple and not too rich; the kind of thing that goes perfectly with a cup of tea by a roaring fire. These biscuits hit the spot at Easter, when we need a little respite from all the chocolate. *Makes 16–18.*

110 g/4 oz unsalted butter,
    room temperature, plus
    extra for greasing
85 g/3 oz caster sugar, plus
    extra for sprinkling
1 medium egg, separated
200 g/7 oz plain flour
½ tsp mixed spice

½ tsp cinnamon
55 g/2 oz currants
finely grated zest of
    1 orange
finely grated zest of
    1 unwaxed lemon
2 tbsp milk

1. Preheat the oven to 200°C/ 400°F/Gas 6. Lightly grease two baking sheets with butter.

2. Beat the butter and sugar together until light and fluffy. Add the egg yolk. Set the white aside for later.

3. Sift the flour and spices over the mixture, add the currants and orange and lemon zests, and mix everything together. Add as much of the milk as you need to make a soft dough.

4. Tip the mixture onto a floured surface and knead with your knuckles until the dough looks smooth.

5. Now roll out the dough, using a floured rolling pin (or a clean wine bottle if that's all you have!), so that it is around 0.5cm/¼in thick. Using a 5cm/2in fluted pastry cutter, stamp out rounds until you have used all the dough.

6. Place the rounds on the prepared baking sheet and bake for 10 minutes. Take the cookies out of the oven, brush with the egg white and sprinkle with the extra sugar. Pop back in the oven and bake for another 10 minutes so they are glistening and golden.

Triple chocolate cookies

These are the ultimate chocolate hit in a cookie and a fantastic way of using up any leftover Easter eggs. You can use any combination of chocolate – I like a mixture of creamy white, smooth milk and intense plain chocolate for the best look and flavour. The cookies are particularly delicious served warm from the oven while still oozing molten chocolate, perhaps accompanied by a scoop of vanilla ice cream. If there are any left, I stack them up and wrap them in coloured paper, tied with ribbon, for my friends and family to take home. *Makes 20.*

200 g/7 oz unsalted butter,
    room temperature
255 g/9 oz caster sugar
125 g/4½ oz muscovado sugar
1 medium egg
1 tsp vanilla extract
45 g/1½ oz cocoa powder
255 g/9 oz plain flour
¾ tsp bicarbonate of soda

2 tbsp milk
55 g/2 oz plain chocolate,
    chopped
55 g/2 oz milk chocolate,
    chopped
55 g/2 oz white chocolate,
    chopped

1. Preheat the oven to 180°C/ 350°F/Gas 4. Line a large baking sheet with greaseproof paper.

2. Cream the butter and both sugars together, beating until pale and fluffy.

3. Add the egg and the vanilla extract. Once they are mixed, sift in the cocoa powder, flour and bicarbonate. The mixture will now seem a little dry, so add the milk and stir until all ingredients are combined. Stir in the chocolate pieces, but take care you don't over-mix at this stage.

4. Drop tablespoonfuls of mixture onto the baking sheet, placing each spoonful about 5cm/2in apart. If you want to make sure the cookies turn out as neat rounds, pop them in the fridge for half an hour or so before baking. But if your mouth is already watering, put the cookies in the preheated oven for 12 minutes and don't worry too much if they begin to ooze into one another as they melt. They will taste just as fantastic, although they may not win any beauty contests.

5. Remove and cool on a wire rack.

Pistachio lime cupcakes

These could be made to look more elegant if drizzled with a simple topping made with icing sugar and lime juice. I couldn't resist doing something kitsch – hence the tiny cupcake garden in the photograph. *Makes 12.*

140 g/5 oz unsalted butter,
 room temperature
285 g/10 oz golden caster
 sugar
120 ml/4 fl oz Greek yoghurt
3 medium eggs
170 g/6 oz self-raising flour
1½ tsp baking powder
55 g/2 oz unsalted pistachio
 nuts, ground
finely grated zest of 1 lime

For the icing
110 g/4 oz unsalted butter,
 room temperature
110 g/4 oz cream cheese,
 room temperature
450 g/1 lb icing sugar
green food colouring paste
sugar flowers, to decorate

1. Preheat the oven to 180°C/ 350°F/Gas 4. Line a 12-hole non-stick muffin tin with paper muffin cases.

2. Beat together the butter and sugar until light and fluffy. Beat the yoghurt into the eggs and then stir into the sugar mixture. Sift the flour and baking powder, add the ground pistachio nuts and lime zest, and then stir into the batter until all the ingredients are incorporated.

3. Spoon the mixture into the paper cases so that they are three-quarters full. Bake the cakes in the centre of the preheated oven for 20–25 minutes until they are firm and

springy to the touch. Remove from the oven and place the cakes on a wire rack to cool. Don't worry if they dip a little in the middle; this is because of the pistachios and they will still taste delicious.

4. To make the icing, cream the butter and cheese in a bowl. Gradually add the icing sugar until you have a good piping/spreading consistency. Dot in a little colouring paste with a skewer and keep mixing until the icing is the shade you like.

5. Using a piping bag with a star nozzle, pipe on the icing. Scatter with the sugar flowers.

White chocolate and raspberry cupcakes

ecadently sumptuous, these are cakes with a sense of occasion. Serve them as a fitting dessert at an elegant dinner party. Makes 12.

140 g/5 oz plain flour
1 tsp baking powder
110 g/4 oz unsalted butter,
    room temperature
110 g/4 oz light brown sugar
2 eggs
1 tsp vanilla extract
½ tsp almond essence
    (optional)
120 ml/4 fl oz milk
110 g/4 oz raspberries

For the filling
140 g/5 oz good-quality
    white chocolate
60 ml/2 fl oz double cream

For the icing
200 g/7 oz raspberries
6 tbsp sugar
1 tbsp water
170 g/6 oz unsalted butter,
    room temperature
340 g/12 oz icing sugar
raspberries or sprinkles,
    to decorate

1. Preheat the oven to 180°C/ 350°F/Gas 4. Line a 12-hole non-stick muffin tin with paper cases.

2. Sift the flour and baking powder into a bowl and set aside.

3. Beat the butter and sugar together until pale and fluffy. Add the eggs, one a time, followed by the vanilla extract and almond essence, if using. Begin to add the flour, alternating with the milk, until all is mixed in. Finally, fold in the raspberries.

4. Spoon the mixture into the paper cases so that they are three-quarters full. Bake the cakes in the centre of the preheated oven for about 20 minutes. Check with a skewer – if the cakes are cooked, the skewer should come out clean. Remove from the oven and place the cakes on a wire rack to cool.

5. To make the filling, melt the chocolate in a bowl set over a saucepan of simmering water or place in a microwave oven for 1 minute. If you use a microwave, stir the chocolate every 20 seconds so it doesn't burn. Once the chocolate has melted, stir in the cream and leave to cool slightly.

6. To make the icing, put the raspberries, sugar and water into a small saucepan and gently bring to the boil. Turn the heat down and simmer for 3 or 4 minutes. Stir occasionally and take care that it doesn't burn. Remove from the heat and leave to cool slightly. Beat the butter in a bowl and then add the icing sugar, a third at a time, beating it in well. Then mix in the raspberry 'jam' you have just made – you may not need it all. Keep any leftover jam – it's delicious spread on bread.

7. Remove a section from the centre of each cake with an apple corer or a small knife, taking care not to go all the way through to the bottom. Fill the cavity with the white-chocolate filling. Using a piping bag, add the raspberry icing in swirls, working from the outside in. Decorate with raspberries or sprinkles.

Biscotti

My mum absolutely adores biscotti. She first tried them on the balcony of a restaurant in a tiny village in Tuscany, gazing up at a wooded mountain as she dipped biscotti into her coffee. This recipe includes a dash of Cointreau, which, though not essential, adds a fragrant zestiness I love. I packaged these in a cellophane bag and tied it with apple-green ribbon as a Mother's Day gift so my mum could be transported back to that Tuscan mountainside. *Makes 15–20.*

255 g/9 oz plain flour, sifted (you may need a little more)
140 g/5 oz golden caster sugar
1 tsp baking powder

170 g/6 oz whole almonds, chopped
170 g/6 oz pistachio nuts, chopped
3 medium eggs
½ tbsp Cointreau

1. Preheat the oven to 180°C/350°F/Gas 4. Line a large baking sheet with greaseproof paper.

2. Mix the flour, sugar, baking powder and nuts in a large bowl until combined.

3. Add the eggs and Cointreau and stir until the mixture comes together in a ball. If the dough seems too wet, add a little extra flour.

4. Divide the dough into two and shape each piece into a long sausage measuring about 20cm/8in long by 7.5cm/3in wide. Place the sausages of dough on the baking sheet and flatten slightly so they are about 2.5cm/1in high.

5. Bake in the centre of the oven for 20 minutes until the dough is golden brown and feels cooked through. Remove from the oven and leave to cool for 15 minutes. Leave the oven on.

6. Place the baked dough on a chopping board. Cut on the diagonal into slices about 1.5cm/½in thick and place them cut side up on the baking sheet.

7. Bake for another 10 minutes, then turn the slices over and bake for another 5 minutes. They should look golden brown and crispy. Remove the biscotti from the oven, place on a wire rack and leave to cool completely.

Crispy nests

This is just about the easiest recipe in the world and gives great satisfaction to little people, who will probably stuff a lot of the mixture into their rosebud mouths. That, of course, is one of the pleasures of making cakes! *Makes 12.*

300 g/11 oz plain chocolate
3 tbsp golden syrup
55 g/2 oz unsalted butter

140 g/5 oz Rice Krispies
25–30 chocolate mini eggs

1. Melt the chocolate in a bowl over a pan of simmering water. (If you're a little person, ask a grown-up to help with this.) Add the butter, cut into small pieces, and stir until melted. Add the golden syrup and stir until it has dissolved.

2. Add the Rice Krispies and stir until they are well mixed into the chocolate. Spoon into paper cases, then make a little dip in the middle of each one with the back of your spoon. Place the crispy nests in the fridge to set.

3. When they are firm, place some chocolate eggs into the dip on the top of each one.

Summer

...succulent strawberries,
raspberries and roses...

When I was a child, summer holidays seemed to stretch ahead of me like a long, meandering road full of promise and rich with possibilities. They were English summers, but I remember many long hot afternoons spent lazing in the garden. I would lie in the glorious sun while I read my book, occasionally rolling over to enjoy the shade under the wonderful cool umbrella of a walnut tree. I loved Edna O'Brien's *The Country Girls* and as I read I would wonder what to 'feck' from the pantry. As my thoughts turned to food, my mum, displaying almost telepathic powers, would emerge from the house carrying a jug of cooling fruit punch accompanied by the lightest lemony biscuits. As their tart tang tingled on my tongue schooldays seemed unimaginably far away.

Seaside trips were always the highlight of the summer holidays. It would seem like the longest journey, but once there it would be bliss. Surrounded by picnic baskets, flasks, books, bats and balls, my sister and I would lie companionably side-by-side and stare out at the turquoise sea which reflected the perfect infinity of sky, bright blue and dotted with puffy clouds. The excitement of the outing would begin with the preparations of the brightly coloured food we'd take with us. Deep purple berries would be flung into icing sugar and rolled under creamy frosting to rest upon a tender crumbly vanilla sponge. Orange cupcakes were piled with a voluptuous froth of meringue frosting that seemed to explode in the mouth. Ice cream cones were filled with sponge and cloaked in creamy vanilla butter cream, then finished with a flake and scattered with hundreds and thousands. Even now, the coconut scent of suntan lotion brings a rush of nostalgia, and I drift back to watch my miniature self rushing to and fro, teasing the sea and asking for it to catch me; loving it and fearing it at the same time. I picture Mummy wrapping me up in a soft sunshine-yellow towel, holding me close and breathing in the heady smell of sand and sea and toddler. Those days seemed to go on and on, melting one into another, as if there was no beginning and would be no end.

When I was growing up in the countryside the big event of the summer was the Norfolk Show and we never felt more poverty stricken than the time our mother confided that she didn't have the money to take us. My sister and I were not to be defeated, however. I rushed down to the kitchen and began blending and beating and whipping up icing while my sister staggered down from the attic laden with box after box. My brother sat, oblivious to it all, lost in his stack of comic books.

The house was soon filled with the scent of vanilla that I breathed in greedily while helping my sister carry a trestle table down the drive where we set up shop. I arranged the sugar-sprinkled cupcakes on a large lilac tray and placed them on the table with the dolls, puzzles and board games we no longer wanted. A few cars passed us before our brother strode down from the house carrying a large hand-painted sign declaring 'Cake and Toy Sale'. Within an hour and a half we had sold out and raised more than enough money for us to go to the Norfolk Show.

Once there, we looked at everything on offer to be sure that every hard-earned penny was spent thoughtfully. We watched the impressive Shire horses pulling carts and the Palominos dancing and prancing around the ring. After watching the showjumping, I persuaded my sister to come and see the tiny wriggling piglets and the angora goats. After much thought, I chose to spend my money on a peg-doll kit and my sister spent hers on a patchwork quilt set. The remaining coins we spent at the Women's Institute stall, where we bought chocolate oat cookies and drank fresh cold milk while watching the cows being judged…

Sunlight dapples the ground ahead as my little girl Kitty and I duck beneath low branches that stretch, tentacle-like, over the river, until we have found the perfect picnic spot – a heart-shaped patch of grass that is partly shaded by a weeping willow. I shake out the red woollen blanket that is a little threadbare in places and still stuck with the dried grass of long-ago picnics. Kitty does her best to smooth out the ridges with her doughy little fingers as I pull each corner tight. Like a magician, Kitty pulls out foil parcels from the basket, arranging them on the blanket in a haphazard fashion. Pastel-coloured macaroons filled with almond butter cream rest next to thickly cut doorsteps of ham sandwich. The crunchy carrot sticks and humus are perilously close to the pecan banana cookies and the voluptuous topping of the lemon meringue cupcake has cracked and crumbled during the journey, but we don't mind. I set out the plates and serve up the home-made lemonade.

Suddenly, Kitty declares with absolute authority, 'Now we must eat! And the Queen says that today we must eat backwards – so cakes and cookies first, then the sandwiches.' 'Okay, your Majesty,' I say, seeing no good reason to argue. 'I am not the Queen,' she replies seriously. 'The Queen lives far away but she sees everything, and she has a baby who looks like a pig!' We fall back laughing at the freedom, gazing up at the blue, blue sky and the crazily shaped clouds that drift above us like puffs of flour masquerading as elves, dinosaurs, boots and witches' faces.

Tiramisu cupcakes

Coffee sponge drenched in Marsala, blanketed in an authentic Italian custard with just a smattering of cocoa powder – wow! Please note, the topping contains raw egg. *Makes 12.*

2 large eggs
120 g/4½ oz light muscovado
    sugar
120 ml/4 fl oz groundnut oil
120 g/4½ oz self-raising flour
1 tsp baking powder
50 ml/2 fl oz espresso or strong
    filter coffee
3–4 tbsp Marsala wine

For the topping
2 egg whites
1 egg yolk
45 g/1½ oz icing sugar
170 g/6 oz mascarpone
grated dark chocolate,
    to decorate

1. Preheat the oven to 180°C/ 350°F/Gas 4. Line a 12-hole non-stick muffin tin with paper muffin cases.

2. Whisk the eggs and sugar together until they become pale in colour, and then gradually add the oil. Sift the flour and baking powder together and add this, a third at a time to the batter, followed by the coffee.

3. Fill the cake cases three-quarters full. Bake the cakes in the centre of the preheated oven for about 20 minutes until the tops feel springy to the touch. Remove and place the cakes on a wire rack to cool. Sprinkle each cake with a teaspoon or two of Marsala.

4. To make the topping, whisk the egg whites until they form stiff peaks. In a separate bowl, whisk the egg yolk with the icing sugar until pale and thick, then add the mascarpone. Once this mixture is smooth, gently fold in the egg whites. Spread about a tablespoon of the mixture on the top of each cupcake and sprinkle with the grated chocolate.

Pistachio rose blossom cakes

The pale elegance of these makes me smile and their slightly chewy texture combined with the moistness of the pistachios makes for a satisfying mouthful. *Makes 12.*

5 large eggs, separated
225 g/8 oz caster sugar
225 g/8 oz pistachio nuts

3 tsp rose water
grated zest of 1 lemon
icing sugar, to decorate

1. Preheat the oven to 170°C/ 325°F/Gas 3. Line a 12-hole non-stick muffin tin with paper muffin cases.

2. Whisk the egg yolks with the caster sugar until light and creamy. Finely grind three-quarters of the pistachio nuts and add them to the egg yolks with the rose water and lemon zest. Stir to combine.

3. Beat the egg whites until stiff and stir 1–2 tablespoons into the egg and pistachio mixture to soften it. Now fold in the rest of the egg whites, keeping as much air in them as possible. Chop the remaining pistachios coarsely.

4. Fill the cake cases generously and top with roughly chopped pistachios. Bake in the preheated oven for about 20 minutes. Remove and place the cakes on a wire rack to cool. Don't worry if they dip a little in the middle; it is due to the pistachios and they will still taste delicious. Sprinkle with icing sugar to decorate.

Strawberries and cream cupcakes

My husband adores these. The ricotta and strawberry filling keeps them light and moist and evokes the flavours of summer. *Makes 12.*

110 g/4 oz unsalted butter,
  room temperature
110 g/4 oz sugar, plus 1 tsp
  to sprinkle on strawberries
2 large eggs
1 tsp vanilla essence
110 g/4 oz plain flour
2 tsp baking powder

1–2 tbsp milk
110 g/4 oz strawberries
85 g/3 oz ricotta cheese
icing sugar (optional),
  to decorate
30 g/1 oz mascarpone
a few extra strawberries,
  sliced

1. Preheat the oven to 180°C/350°F/Gas 4. Line a 12-hole non-stick muffin tin with paper muffin cases.

2. Cream the butter and sugar together until light and fluffy. Add the eggs, one by one, then the vanilla.

3. Sift the flour and baking powder into a separate bowl. Fold the flour into the butter and sugar mixture, adding a tablespoon or two of milk to keep the batter soft.

4. Roughly chop the strawberries into another bowl and sprinkle with the teaspoon of sugar. Stir in the ricotta and mix gently so that the strawberries are fairly evenly distributed.

5. Put 1 flat tablespoonful of cake batter into each paper case so it is about one-third full. Make sure the mixture covers the base of the case. Next, add 1 tablespoon of the strawberry mixture, levelling it so that it reaches the edges. Finish with another 1 tablespoon of the cake batter to seal in the pink centre.

6. Bake the cakes in the centre of the preheated oven for about 20 minutes until the tops feel springy to the touch. Remove and place the cakes on a wire rack to cool.

7. When the cakes are cool, sprinkle the tops with sifted icing sugar, if liked, add a small teaspoon of the mascarpone and a slice of strawberry.

Strawberry crumb cupcakes

I find it easiest to use a silicone muffin tray to mould the cupcakes, as it makes it easier to turn them out. The creamy strawberry taste of these reminds me of the home-made ice cream I used to eat at a friend's farm when I was a child. *Makes 12.*

For the base
12 digestive biscuits
2 tsp demerara sugar
110 g/4 oz butter, melted

For the cakes
110 g/4 oz unsalted butter,
    room temperature
110 g/4 oz caster sugar
2 large eggs
110 g/4 oz self-raising flour
1 tsp baking powder
1 tsp vanilla extract

For the filling
400 g/14 oz strawberries
12 tbsp sugar
2 tbsp water

For the icing
55 g/2 oz unsalted butter,
    room temperature
55 g/2 oz cream cheese,
    room temperature
225 g/8 oz icing sugar, sifted
sugar flowers, to decorate
    (optional)

1. Preheat the oven to 180°C/ 350°F/Gas 4. Line a 12-hole non-stick muffin tin with paper cases.

2. Put the digestives in a plastic bag and crush with a rolling pin until fine. Put them in a bowl, stir in the demerara sugar, then the melted butter and mix well. Press firmly into the base of each paper case.

3. To make the cakes, cream the butter and sugar together until fluffy. Add the eggs, then the flour, baking powder and vanilla. Drop 1 generous tablespoon of mixture onto the crumb base in each case and bake for 20 minutes. Cool on a wire rack.

4. To make the jam filling, put the strawberries, sugar and water into a pan and gently bring to the boil. Turn down the heat and simmer for 3–4 minutes. Stir occasionally, taking care that the mixture doesn't burn. Remove from the heat and leave to cool slightly. Remove the centre of each cake with a small knife or an apple corer and fill with a teaspoon of the 'jam' you have just made.

5. To make the icing, whisk the butter with the cream cheese and icing sugar. Add enough of the remaining 'jam' to make a pleasing colour and use this to ice the cakes with the aid of a palette knife.

Bounty cupcakes

My favourite childhood chocolate bar reinvented as a cupcake – what's not to love? *Makes 12.*

110 g/4 oz unsalted butter, room temperature
110 g/4 oz caster sugar
2 large eggs
12 tbsp coconut milk
110 g/4 oz desiccated coconut
140 g/5 oz self-raising flour
1 tsp baking powder

For the icing
110 g/4 oz chocolate, plain or milk
2 tbsp soured cream
4 tsp caster sugar

1. Preheat the oven to 170°C/ 325°F/Gas 3. Line a 12-hole non-stick muffin tin with paper muffin cases.

2. Cream the butter and sugar together until light, pale and fluffy. Add the eggs, one by one, then the coconut milk and desiccated coconut. Sift the flour and baking powder into the mixture and fold in gently.

3. Divide the mixture between the paper cases. Bake in the preheated oven for 15–20 minutes until firm and springy to the touch. Place the cakes on a wire rack to cool.

4. Meanwhile, prepare the icing. Melt the chocolate in a bowl over a pan of simmering water or put it in a microwave for 90 seconds or so. When melted, remove from the heat and stir in the soured cream and sugar. Whisk to combine and spoon the icing over the cooled cupcakes.

Courgette cupcakes

These were an absolutely massive hit when I served them at a friend's barbecue. Just don't tell the kids what's in them. I didn't and they ate them all, making a pain-free way to get your children to eat more veg. *Makes 20.*

170 g/6 oz courgettes
2 large eggs
125 ml/4 fl oz sunflower oil
140 g/5 oz soft brown sugar
225 g/8 oz self-raising flour
½ tsp bicarbonate of soda
½ tsp baking powder

For the icing
200 g/7 oz cream cheese,
   room temperature
110 g/4 oz icing sugar, sifted
juice of 1 lime
green food colouring paste
pink rose petals, to decorate
1 egg white, to decorate
caster sugar, to decorate

1. Preheat the oven to 180°C/350°F/Gas 4. Line two 12-hole non-stick muffin tins with 20 paper muffin cases.

2. Rinse the courgettes and grate them coarsely. Press them in a sieve to squeeze out excess moisture.

3. Beat the eggs, oil and sugar together until creamy. Sieve in the flour, bicarbonate and baking powder and beat well. Mix in the grated courgette.

4. Spoon the mixture into the paper cases. Bake the cakes in the centre of the preheated oven for about 20 minutes until firm and springy to the touch. Remove and place the cakes on a wire rack to cool.

5. To make the icing, beat the cream cheese until it is smooth and add the icing sugar. Beat well to combine, then add the lime juice and a drop of green food colouring paste.

6. Gently rinse the rose petals in water and lay them on kitchen paper to dry. Lightly whisk the egg white and paint it gently onto the petals. Sprinkle over a little caster sugar and leave to dry.

7. When the cakes have cooled, use a palette knife to spread on the icing, and then decorate with the sugar rose petals.

Orange, raspberry and yoghurt cupcakes

These cupcakes consist of a deliciously damp sponge with a jewel-like raspberry buried at the heart. If you like, you can decorate them with pretty rice paper flowers *Makes 12–16.*

225 g/8 oz plain flour, plus
   1 tbsp
2 tsp baking powder
55 g/2 oz ground almonds
2 large eggs
90 ml/3 fl oz sunflower oil
250 ml/8½ fl oz low-fat
   Greek yoghurt
250 g/8½ oz sugar

grated zest and juice of
   1 orange
approx. 24 raspberries

For the icing
500 g/1 lb 2 oz icing sugar
75 ml/2½ fl oz Greek
   yoghurt
rice paper flowers, to decorate

1. Preheat the oven to 180°C/ 350°F/Gas 4. Line a 12-hole non-stick muffin tin with paper muffin cases.

2. Sift the flour and baking powder together and add the ground almonds.

3. In a large bowl, mix the eggs, oil, yoghurt and sugar together. Add the dry ingredients, followed by the orange juice and zest, and mix until thoroughly combined.

4. Spoon the mixture into the cases so they are half full. Dust the raspberries with the tablespoon of flour (to prevent them sinking) and add a couple to each cake case. Add the rest of the cake batter.

5. Bake the cakes for 25 minutes until they are springy to the touch. Remove and place the cakes on a wire rack to cool. If you have leftover mixture, make another batch, as before.

6. Next make the icing. Sift the icing sugar into a large bowl and stir in the yoghurt. The consistency should be thick but easy to spread. If it isn't, add a drop or two of water.

7. When the thickness seems right, coat the top of each cake with about half a tablespoon of icing, spreading it to reach the edges. Leave plain or decorate with rice paper flowers or extra raspberries, if you wish.

Lemon meringue cupcakes

When I was a little girl, lemon meringue pie was the dessert that my mum was always willing to make. Even if the larder seemed almost empty, she would somehow manage to find the ingredients. *Makes 12.*

110 g/4 oz cream cheese,
  room temperature
1 tbsp icing sugar
1 tbsp fresh lemon juice
110 g/4 oz unsalted butter
110 g/4 oz sugar
2 large eggs
110 g/4 oz self-raising flour,
  sifted
1 tsp baking powder

For the lemon curd
85 g/3 oz unsalted butter
3 tbsp fresh lemon juice
2 large eggs
2 large egg yolks
110 g/4 oz caster sugar
grated rind of 2 lemons

For the meringue
2 large egg whites
225 g/8 oz caster sugar

1. Preheat the oven to 180°C/ 350°F/Gas 4. Line a 12-hole non-stick muffin tin with paper cases.

2. Whisk the cream cheese, icing sugar and lemon juice together in a medium-sized bowl and set aside. Cream the butter and sugar together until light and fluffy. Add the eggs, one by one, then the sifted flour and baking powder. Gently stir the cream cheese into the batter.

3. Divide the mixture between the paper cases, but don't fill more than half full. Bake in the centre of the preheated oven for 20 minutes until cooked inside. Check by inserting a skewer into the cakes. If the cakes

are cooked it should come out clean. Remove and turn the cakes onto a wire rack to cool.

4. Prepare the lemon curd. Put the butter and lemon juice in a pan over a medium heat until the butter melts. In a bowl, whisk the eggs, egg yolks and sugar together until blended. Continue whisking as you slowly incorporate the hot butter and lemon mixture into the eggs, then pour back into the pan. Cook over a medium heat, stirring with a wooden spoon, until the mixture reaches boiling point and thickens – this should take about 5 minutes. Remove from the heat, strain into a bowl and add the grated lemon rind.

5. To make the meringue, beat the egg whites until they form soft peaks. Add the sugar a little at a time until it is all incorporated.

6. Using an apple corer, remove the centre of each cupcake. Fill with lemon curd and spread a layer over the top of the cakes.

7. Preheat the oven to 170°C/ 325°F/Gas 3. Using a small spatula, swirl some meringue mixture over the top of each cake to seal in the lemon curd. Put back in the preheated oven to bake for another 15 minutes. Any unused lemon curd can be stored in the freezer for up to 3 months.

Blueberry clouds

The biscuit base of the cakes clings to a vanilla sponge topped with cream cheese icing and filled with blueberry jam. When my niece first saw these she named them blueberry clouds and they have been called this ever since. *Makes 12.*

For the base
12 digestive biscuits
2 tsp demerara sugar
110 g/4 oz melted butter

For the cakes
200 g/7 oz cream cheese
2 tsp lemon juice
1 tbsp icing sugar
110 g/4 oz unsalted butter,
    room temperature
110 g/4 oz caster sugar
2 large eggs
110 g/4 oz self-raising flour

1 tsp vanilla
1 tsp baking powder

For the filling
3 tbsp blueberry jam

For the icing
170 g/6 oz unsalted butter,
    room temperature
170 g/6 oz cream cheese,
    room temperature
500 g/1 lb 2 oz icing sugar
purple food colouring
    paste

1. Preheat the oven to 180°C/ 350°F/Gas 4. Line a 12-hole non-stick muffin tin with paper muffin cases.

2. First make the base. Place the digestives in a plastic bag and bash them with a rolling pin until they resemble fine breadcrumbs. Put them in a bowl, stir in the demerara sugar, then the melted butter and mix well. Press firmly into the base of each paper case.

3. Whisk the cream cheese in a bowl with the lemon juice and sifted icing sugar until combined. Set aside.

4. To make the cakes, whisk the butter and sugar until fluffy. Add the eggs, followed by the vanilla, flour and baking powder. When thoroughly combined, stir in the cream cheese mixture that was set aside earlier.

5. Drop 1 tablespoon of cake mixture onto the crumb base in each paper case and bake in the oven for 20 minutes. Cool on a wire rack.

6. Remove the centre of each cake with an apple corer and fill with about a teaspoon of jam.

7. Cream together the butter and cream cheese for the icing and beat in the icing sugar. Add a dot of food colouring to make the icing a lilac colour. Spread a thin layer of icing over the top of each cake.

Farmhouse biscuits

These are like the reassuringly wholesome biscuits we used to be served by the farmer's wife at the farm where my sister kept her horse. *Makes about 20.*

110 g/4 oz unsalted butter,
  room temperature
100 g/3½ oz light brown sugar
75 g/2½ oz crunchy peanut
  butter
1 egg
55 g/2 oz plain flour

½ tsp baking powder
½ tsp ground cinnamon
170 g/6 oz muesli
55 g/2 oz raisins
55 g/2 oz shelled walnuts,
  chopped

1. Preheat the oven to 180°C/350°F/Gas 4. Grease a large baking sheet.

2. Using a wooden spoon, beat the butter and sugar together until light and fluffy. Beat in the peanut butter and the egg.

3. Sift the flour, baking powder and cinnamon over the peanut butter mixture and stir well to blend. Add the muesli, raisins and walnuts and mix again. Taste for sweetness – you might want to add more sugar, depending on the sweetness of the muesli.

4. Drop tablespoons of the mixture onto the baking sheet, leaving about 2.5cm/1in between them, and press each one down with the back of the spoon.

5. Bake for about 15 minutes until golden. Remove with a spatula and leave to cool on a wire rack.

Pecan banana cookies

The granola in this recipe makes for a lovely rustic texture, which really brings out the warm banana flavour. *Makes 12.*

110 g/4 oz flour
½ tsp bicarbonate of soda
½ tsp baking powder
½ tsp salt
55 g/2 oz unsalted butter,
  room temperature
110 g/4 oz soft brown sugar

55 g/2 oz granulated sugar
1 tsp vanilla extract
1 egg
1 banana, mashed
170 g/6 oz granola
45 g/1½ oz pecans

1. Preheat the oven to 170°C/ 325°F/Gas 3. Have a large ungreased baking sheet ready.

2. Mix the flour, bicarbonate, baking powder and salt together in a small bowl. Cream the butter, sugars and vanilla in a large bowl until light and fluffy. Then mix in the egg, followed by the flour mixture, and stir to blend all the ingredients. Mix in the mashed banana, granola and nuts and make sure everything is well combined.

3. Drop rounded tablespoons of mixture onto the baking sheet, leaving space for them to expand. Bake for 10–12 minutes or until just golden on top.

4. Remove the cookies from the oven and leave them to cool on the baking sheet for 5 minutes before transferring to a wire rack.

Orange polenta cookies

These are at their most delicious when dipped in a bowl of syllabub. Perfect for a picnic by the river on a summer's day. *Makes 12–15.*

85 g/3 oz unsalted butter, room temperature
140 g/5 oz granulated sugar, plus extra to sprinkle
grated zest of 1 orange

½ tsp vanilla extract
1 large egg
140 g/5 oz plain flour
55 g/2 oz polenta

1. Preheat the oven to 170°C/325°F/Gas 3. You will need a large lightly greased baking sheet.

2. Cream the butter and sugar, beating together until light and fluffy. Add the orange zest and vanilla and beat the egg into the mixture. Add the flour and polenta and stir to combine.

3. Take walnut-sized pieces of the mixture and roll into balls. Place the balls on the baking sheet, flatten lightly and sprinkle with a little granulated sugar.

4. Bake for 12–15 minutes until the cookies are golden around the edges. Remove them from the oven and place on a wire rack to cool.

Chocolate oat cookies

These are deeply satisfying, with their rich chocolate-y-ness nicely balanced by the healthy oats. *Makes about 20.*

60 ml/2 fl oz sunflower oil
85 g/3 oz unsalted butter,
    room temperature
110 g/4 oz caster sugar
110 g/4 oz light brown sugar
1 egg
½ tsp vanilla extract

110 g/4 oz porridge oats
170 g/6 oz rice flour
½ tsp baking powder
½ tsp bicarbonate of soda
170 g/6 oz chocolate, mixture
    of plain and milk

1. Preheat the oven to 180°C/ 350°F/Gas 4. Lightly grease a baking sheet.

2. Mix the oil, butter and sugars together and beat until smooth. Beat in the egg and vanilla, followed by the oats.

3. In another bowl, sift the flour with the baking powder and bicarbonate. Mix the flour into the oats mixture and beat with a wooden spoon until thoroughly combined. Chop the chocolate into small pieces and add to the mixture.

4. Drop heaped spoonfuls of the mixture onto the baking sheet, leaving 5cm/2in between each one. I like to put them in the fridge at this point for an hour or two to firm up before cooking.

5. Bake for 10 minutes until the cookies are set on top but still gooey in the centre. Leave to cool on the tray for 5–10 minutes before transferring to a wire rack.

Tropical cookies

This recipe was one of my grandma's favourites and we always used to make these cookies on her birthday. They have a unique flavour and an almost cake-like texture, due to the pineapple, and they are surprisingly moist for cookies. *Makes 20.*

225 g/8 oz plain flour
½ tsp bicarbonate of soda
½ tsp baking powder
pinch of salt
55 g/2 oz unsalted butter,
    room temperature
170 g/6 oz soft brown sugar

1 egg
170 g/6 oz canned coconut
    cream
170 g/6 oz pineapple cubes,
    chopped
45 g/1½ oz desiccated coconut

1. Preheat the oven to 170°C/ 325°F/Gas 3. You will need a large lightly greased baking sheet.

2. Mix the flour, bicarbonate, baking powder and salt together in a small bowl. In a large bowl, cream the butter and sugar together until light and fluffy. Then add the egg and coconut cream, stir well and add the flour mixture, blending everything together. Stir in the chopped pineapple and coconut.

3. Drop rounded tablespoons of mixture onto the baking sheet, leaving space between each cookie. Bake for 10–12 minutes or until just golden on top. Remove from the oven and leave to cool on the baking sheet for 5 minutes before transferring to a wire rack.

99 Cones with flakes

These appeal to the child in me. They are simple to make and yet they really have the wow factor. Use the cheapest vanilla for this recipe, as it will give the most authentic flavour. *Makes about 12.*

12 flat-based ice-cream cones
110 g/4 oz unsalted butter,
   room temperature
110 g/4 oz caster sugar
3 large eggs
110 g/4 oz self-raising flour
1 tsp baking powder
1 tsp vanilla extract
4 chocolate flakes, cut into 3

For the icing
225 g/8 oz unsalted butter,
   room temperature
450 g/1 lb icing sugar, sifted
2 tsp vanilla extract

1. Preheat the oven to 180°C/ 350°F/Gas 4. Cut 12 squares of foil, each measuring 15cm/6in, and press them into 12 regular muffin tin holes, letting the foil hang over the edges. Place an ice-cream cone in each piece of foil and wrap the foil around the cone to hold it in place.

2. Cream the butter and sugar together until pale and fluffy. Beat in the eggs, one at a time, until well incorporated. Sift the flour and baking powder together and add this a third at a time to the batter. Add the vanilla extract.

3. Spoon the mixture into the cones, filling to just below the top of the cone. Place in the centre of the oven and bake for about 20 minutes so that the cakes are springy to the touch and a skewer inserted into the centre comes out clean. Place on a wire rack and leave to cool.

4. Make the icing. Beat the butter so that it is pale and creamy and add the icing sugar and the vanilla.

5. Using a piping bag with a star-shaped nozzle, pipe the icing onto the cupcakes to create a Mr Whippy effect. Add a chocolate flake to each one.

Gypsy creams

I remember this name from my childhood so I went about re-inventing them. I think my version does the name justice. Filled with chocolate ganache, they make a sophisticated treat. *Makes 24 biscuits (12 sandwiches).*

140 g/5 oz unsalted butter,
   room temperature
55 g/2 oz soft dark brown
   sugar
1 egg, lightly beaten
1 tsp vanilla extract
225 g/8 oz plain flour
30 g/1 oz cocoa powder
½ tsp baking powder
a pinch of salt

For the filling
250 g/9 oz plain chocolate,
   broken into pieces
pinch of salt
3 tbsp caster sugar
300 ml/10 fl oz soured cream

1. Preheat the oven to 170°C/325°F/Gas 3. You will need a large lightly greased baking sheet.

2. Cream the butter and sugar together until pale and fluffy, then add the egg and vanilla extract. Stir well. Mix together the flour, cocoa powder, baking powder and salt and add to the butter mixture, stirring until well combined.

3. Take a heaped teaspoon of the mixture and roll it into a ball, then flatten with the palm of your hand and place on the baking sheet.

Repeat until all the mixture is used up. Bake for 20 minutes until the biscuits look cooked through.

4. To make the filling, melt the chocolate in a bowl over a pan of simmering water or by putting it in the microwave for 20 seconds. Whisk in the salt, sugar and soured cream. Allow the filling to cool until it is thick enough to spread – put it in the fridge to speed up the process.

5. Spread the filling over half the biscuits and then top with the rest to make sandwiches.

Pastel macaroons

These delicately scented, pastel-coloured macaroons look beautiful and their chewy texture makes them hard to resist. *Makes 20.*

For the macaroons
2 large egg whites
15 g/½ oz caster sugar
125 g/4½ oz icing sugar
75 g/2½ oz ground almonds

For the filling
125 g/4½ oz unsalted butter,
   room temperature
250 g/8½ oz icing sugar, sifted
55 g/2 oz ground almonds

For the flavours
1 tsp rose water
pink food colouring paste
or
1 tsp lemon oil
yellow food colouring paste
or
1 tsp orange oil
orange food colouring paste
or
4 tbsp lavender buds
lilac food colouring paste
or
use ground pistachios instead
   of almonds
green food colouring paste

1. Preheat the oven to 180°C/ 350°F/Gas 4. Line a large baking sheet with greaseproof paper.

2. Whisk the egg whites until stiff, not dry. Sprinkle with caster sugar and continue whisking until stiff again. Stir the icing sugar together with the ground almonds and then gently mix into the egg whites. Add a minute amount of colour paste and your flavouring of choice (see overleaf for methods).

3. Using a piping bag and a plain 1-cm nozzle, pipe small rounds of the macaroon mixture onto the greaseproof paper. Bake in the oven for 10–12 minutes until the macaroons are set but not dried out. Remove from the oven and allow to cool on the paper.

4. Cream the butter and sugar for the filling before slowly adding the ground nuts. Carry on beating to achieve a creamy texture, before adding your choice of flavour and colour.

Flavours

Rose – add half a teaspoon of rose water to the macaroon mixture and half to the filling. Add a dot of pink colouring paste to each.

Lemon – add half a teaspoon of lemon oil to the macaroon mixture and half a teaspoon to the filling. Add a dot of yellow colouring paste to each.

Orange – add half a teaspoon of orange oil to the macaroon mixture and half a teaspoon to the filling. Add a dot of orange colouring paste to each.

Lavender – add 2 tablespoons of lavender buds to the caster sugar and another 2 tablespoons to the icing sugar for the filling and leave to infuse overnight. Sift both sugars separately and add a dot of lilac colour paste to the filling and the macaroon mixture.

Pistachio – swap almonds for ground pistachios in the macaroon mixture and filling (grind in a food processor with the icing sugar). Add a dot of green paste to each.

Autumn

...toffee apples, pumpkins,
sugar and spice...

I remember travelling home from school in autumn when the nights were drawing in. Stepping off the bus, bat-blind in the country darkness, I would forge ahead, bitter wind whipping at my cheeks. The road is long and winds ahead, unpredictable as a snake. I hear the drumming sound of water falling from the gnarled trees that line my path; they seem to bend and sway in a manner all too human. I half grope my way up the long straight drive and as I get nearer to The Mill I can make out its silhouette. The shapes come into sharper focus as the light from windows and doors floods out to welcome me home.

Stepping through the door I am enveloped in the heady smell of Mum's baking. The aroma is of burnt sugar and buttery sponge – it is one of my favourites: sticky toffee pudding. I gulp down my supper at lightning speed, so eager am I to get to dessert. When it comes, it is molten hot, bubbling like a volcano under a pale puddle of thick cream. I approach gingerly, wary of searing the roof of my mouth, and begin by tasting only the sponge and working around to the sauce so it is just the right temperature. The pudding is dense and the sauce rich and thick as it coats my tongue. I am in heaven.

When I lie awake at night and sleep is out of reach, my mind fills with sweet and tempting combinations – delicate coconut sponge fringed with bitter chocolate blanket, banana buns hollowed out and filled with dreamy toffee, then cream, and topped with fresh banana, like banoffee pie. These are the thoughts that make me unable to surrender to sleep. At times the pull is too strong and I have to creep out of bed and fumble my way down the shadowy hall to my kitchen. I put the oven on and forget what time it is as I lose myself in my creative delights, measuring and pouring and experimenting, until I fall sticky and exhausted back into bed and dream of cookie towers and cupcake mountains....

Halloween is just around the corner and a low-lying mist creeps up the edges of my windows. It inspires me to create all kinds of ghostly confections. When I was a child we would combine Halloween with Guy Fawkes Night, which meant we could indulge in setting off fireworks as well as dressing up. I make a bonfire cake covered in chocolate mint sticks and sparklers to give it added flair. I love biscuits shaped like bloody hands, the jam sandwiched between them just beginning to ooze out. Spooky ghost cakes, with their sugary tender texture, are coated in whipped white icing swirled into a spectre-like peak, with a couple of currants making out the hollow eyes. Chocolate brownies can be sliced into crumbling tombstones and set into a cake board covered with desiccated coconut that has been dyed moss green. Carve some ghosts out of marshmallow and prepare to horrify. What would Halloween be without pumpkins? Use up any left-over pale amber flesh in spicy pumpkin cupcakes with a bright orange top and inky black features scowling up at you.

Now I see autumn as if for the first time through my daughter's eyes, as the lush green treetops turn to amber and coral. Deep russet canopies the avenue as Kitty and I stroll arm in arm, our feet throwing up billowing clouds of gold and brown. When we step inside our faces are pink and cheerful from the nip in the air. We feel like snuggling on the sofa and we need some cosy food too – double chocolate cookies washed down with a cold crisp glass of milky goodness do the trick.

Nightfall is greedily eating up all the scenery, but then the great big moon rises up from nowhere, puffed up and proud and revelling in her full-bodied dimensions. She is impressive and we are riveted. We make a plan but more feasting is required. We cream butter until it is soft and silky, then add dark sticky sugar. Kitty cracks the eggs very carefully, one at a time, but some shell drops into the bowl. I try to remove it, first with the old worn wooden spoon, then with my fingers, but it has a mind of its own and slides away, always one step ahead, like a cotton reel tantalizing a kitten. Eventually I fish it out and we are laughing at the futility of it all   we wouldn't have minded or even noticed had it been in our slice. Now we add the flour, handfuls at a time (Kitty's idea). Her hands are so small it takes some time. We stir in spiky ginger and soothing honey, then turn the lot into a battered square cake tin. When it has baked and cooled just a little, we cut it into great wodges and wrap them in a red gingham tea towel.

We head out to the garden, which stretches out like a wild forest in the indigo night. I carry an old wool blanket and spread it under the biggest tree. We lie down, stare up at the moon, and agree that this is the way life should be.

Pumpkin cupcakes

When my daughter was very small she used to call hollowed-out pumpkins monkeys! These cakes are simple to make and they look sensational. *Makes 12.*

2 large eggs
170 g/6 oz dark muscovado
   sugar
160 ml/5½ fl oz sunflower oil
1 tsp vanilla extract
100 g/3½ oz self-raising flour
1 tsp cinnamon
55 g/2 oz pecans, roughly
   chopped
55 g/2 oz sultanas
100 g/3½ oz pumpkin or
   butternut squash, grated

For the icing
450 g/1 lb icing sugar
110 g/4 oz unsalted butter,
   room temperature
110 g/4 oz cream cheese,
   room temperature
juice and grated rind of
   1 orange
orange food colouring paste
48 black 'bat' sprinkles (see
   Suppliers, page 160),
   to decorate

1. Preheat the oven to 170°C/325°F/Gas 3. Line a 12-hole non-stick muffin tin with paper muffin cases.

2. Beat the eggs in a bowl with the sugar for a couple of minutes, then add the oil and vanilla. Fold in the flour and cinnamon, followed by the nuts, sultanas and pumpkin.

3. Divide the mixture between the paper cases. Bake in the centre of the preheated oven for 20–25 minutes. Remove and turn the cakes out onto a wire rack to cool.

4. To make the icing, sift the icing sugar into a bowl. Mix in the butter, cream cheese and orange juice and rind. Add a couple of drops of orange colouring so as to give a bright pumpkin colour.

5. When the cakes are cool, put some icing into a piping bag and pipe onto each cake. Pipe from top to bottom on either side of the cake, using a star nozzle. Then pipe from top to bottom two or three times again to fill in the middle. I used bat sprinkles to create the eyes and mouth.

Sticky toffee pecan cupcakes

Instead of icing these cakes, you can serve them straight from the oven with the warm sauce drenching them and perhaps a puddle of cream on the side. *Makes 18.*

200 g/7 oz dates, chopped
140 g/5 oz unsalted butter,
    room temperature
170 g/6 oz dark brown sugar
2 eggs
170 g/6 oz plain flour
1½ tsp baking powder

100 g/3½ oz pecan nuts,
    chopped
4 tbsp milk

For the toffee sauce
140 g/5 oz unsalted butter
140 g/5 oz dark brown sugar

1. Preheat the oven to 180°C/ 350°F/Gas 4. Line a 12-hole non-stick muffin tin with paper cases.

2. Put the dates in a bowl and pour in about 150 ml/5 fl oz of boiling water. Leave them to soak for about 20 minutes, by which time the dates will have absorbed most of the water.

3. Cream the butter and sugar together in a large bowl. Once the mixture has lightened in colour and texture, beat in the eggs, one at a time. Sift the flour and baking powder into the mixture and add the nuts. Pour in the milk, then drain the dates and add them to the mixture.

4. By now the batter will be very lumpy, which is just as it should be. Spoon into the paper cases so they are two-thirds full and bake in the preheated oven for 20–25 minutes. Check with a skewer – if the cakes are done it should come out clean.

5. In the meantime, make the toffee sauce. Gently melt the butter in a pan, then add the sugar. Keep stirring over a low to medium heat for 5–10 minutes until the mixture begins to bubble and thicken up. When the sauce turns a delicious toffee colour, it is cooked. Take off the heat and leave to cool slightly before pouring onto the cupcakes. Don't leave it too long, though, or it will get too stiff to pour.

Chocolate frosted toffee cupcakes

These have a lovely caramel flavour that goes perfectly with the chocolate frosting. *Makes 12.*

75 g/2½ oz unsalted butter,
room temperature
140 g/5 oz dark muscovado
sugar
2 large eggs, whites only
140 g/5 oz plain flour
½ tsp bicarbonate of soda
1 tsp baking powder
225 ml/8 fl oz buttermilk

(or full-fat milk with 1 tbsp
vinegar or lemon juice)

For the icing
60 ml/2 fl oz whipping cream
1 tbsp unsalted butter
170 g/6 oz milk chocolate,
chopped
½ tsp vanilla extract

1. Preheat the oven to 170°C/ 325°F/Gas 3. Line a 12-hole non-stick muffin tin with paper cases.

2. Using a wooden spoon, blend the butter with the sugar. This will not cream as well as a usual sponge recipe as there is twice as much sugar as fat, so don't spend too long on this stage before adding the egg whites (un-whisked).

3. Sift the flour, bicarbonate and baking powder into a separate bowl. Add half the flour mixture to the butter and sugar, mix well and add half the buttermilk or milk mixture – the acid is needed to set off the raising agent in the bicarbonate. Then add the rest of the flour, and lastly the remaining milk.

4. Divide the mixture between the paper cases. Bake in the centre of the preheated oven for 20 minutes. Remove and turn the cakes out onto a wire rack to cool.

5. Meanwhile, make the icing. Heat the cream and butter in a medium pan over a low heat until the butter is melted and the cream is hot, but not boiling. Remove from the heat and add the chocolate. Leave for a minute so that the chocolate starts to soften and turn to threads. Stir in the vanilla and whisk until the chocolate is well mixed in and the icing has a lovely shiny glaze.

6. Spread a thick layer of icing over the cakes – you will need about 1 tablespoon for each cake. If the icing is too runny, leave it to cool for 10 minutes.

Chocolate brownie cemetery

These are not as soft as some brownies, but ideal for making these tombstones! If the brownies are too squidgy in the middle to hold their shape, just use the outsides for the stones and serve the rest separately. *Makes 12–15.*

400 g/14 oz dark chocolate,
　　broken into small pieces
375 g/13 oz unsalted butter,
　　room temperature
500 g/1 lb 2 oz sugar
6 large eggs, beaten
225 g/8 oz flour
2 tsp vanilla extract

For the decoration
green food colouring paste
desiccated coconut
icing sugar
black extra food colouring
　　paste
5–7 white marshmallows

1. Preheat the oven to 170°C/ 325°F/Gas 3. Grease a 23 x 30cm/ 9 x 12in baking tin and line it with baking parchment.

2. Melt the chocolate in a bowl over a pan of simmering water or in a microwave – be careful not to burn it if you use a microwave.

3. Cream the butter and sugar together until light and fluffy, then add the melted chocolate and beat well. Mix in the eggs and beat thoroughly before adding the flour and vanilla.

4. Pour into the baking tin, smooth with a spatula and bake in the centre of the oven for 25–30 minutes. They should look dry on the top but still be a little uncooked in the middle –

they will continue cooking as they cool. Take the tin out and leave the brownies to cool.

5. Once the brownies are cool, cut them into tombstone shapes with a sharp knife. Mix a dab of green colouring with a teaspoon of water and use this to colour the coconut. Then create a layer of coconut 'grass' on the serving plate.

6. Mix the icing sugar with a dab of black colouring and a few drops of water to give a piping consistency. Using a plain nozzle, pipe 'RIP' and crosses on the tombstones and arrange them in the dish. Put dots of black colouring in the marshmallows to make eyes and tuck the 'ghosts' behind the tombstones.

Toffee apple cupcakes

I love the way the sharpness of the cake is set off by the buttery toffee topping. I use Cox's apples from my garden, but if you prefer something less tart, substitute with a sweeter apple. I do think it is worth obtaining some lolly sticks for the complete toffee-apple look. *Makes 12.*

110 g/4 oz unsalted butter,
   room temperature
110 g/4 oz demerara sugar
2 large eggs
170 g/6 oz apple, peeled,
   cored and chopped
110 g/4 oz self-raising flour
1 tsp baking powder

For the toffee coating
25 hard toffees
7–10 tbsp milk
12 lolly sticks, to decorate

1. Preheat the oven to 180°C/ 350°F/Gas 4. Line a 12-hole non-stick muffin tin with paper muffin cases.

2. Cream the butter and sugar together – the mixture won't go as pale and creamy as usual due to the coarse grain of the sugar. Stir in the eggs, followed by the chopped apple. Sift in the flour and baking powder.

3. Divide the mixture between the paper cases and bake the cakes in the preheated oven for 20 minutes until

the tops feel springy to the touch. Remove the cupcakes and leave to cool on a wire rack.

4. To make the coating, place the toffees in a pan with 7 tablespoons of milk and warm gently over a low heat. Stir constantly to make a smooth toffee topping, adding more milk if needed.

5. Slowly pour the topping over the cakes to coat them thickly. Push a lolly stick into each cake.

Marmalade cupcakes

This is a simple recipe with a classic old-fashioned flavour. My mother often served these for afternoon tea. *Makes 12.*

110 g/4 oz unsalted butter,
    room temperature
110 g/4 oz sugar
2 eggs
110 g/4 oz self-raising flour
½ tsp baking powder
1 tbsp marmalade

zest of 1 orange, finely grated
juice of 1 orange

For the icing
75–100 g/3–4 oz icing sugar
1 tbsp orange juice

1. Preheat the oven to 180°C/ 350°F/Gas 4. Line a 12-hole non-stick muffin tin with paper muffin cases.

2. Cream the butter and sugar together until pale and fluffy. Beat in the eggs one at a time. Sift the flour and baking powder together and add this a third at a time to the batter. Then add the marmalade and zest and juice of the orange.

3. Spoon into the paper cases and bake in the centre of the preheated oven for about 20 minutes. The cakes should be springy to the touch and a skewer inserted into the centre should come out clean. Place on a wire rack and leave to cool.

4. Sift 75 g/3 oz of the icing sugar into a bowl and add the orange juice. You may need to mix in a little more icing sugar to achieve a spreading consistency. Use a palette knife to spread the icing over the cakes and allow to set. Decorate as you fancy.

Beet-rose cupcakes

These beetroot cupcakes have a satisfyingly complex flavour, with a faint earthiness that contrasts with the toasty taste of hazelnuts. To create the rose effect, use a star-shaped nozzle and start piping from the inside and work your way out to the edge. *Makes 12.*

3 large eggs, separated
2 tbsp milk
100 ml/3½ fl oz groundnut or
   sunflower oil
110 g/4 oz golden or white
   caster sugar
100 g/3½ oz plain flour
1 tsp baking powder
85 g/3 oz raw beetroot, grated
55 g/2 oz hazelnuts, roasted
   and chopped
½ tsp cinnamon

For the icing
110 g/4 oz unsalted butter,
   room temperature
110 g/4 oz cream cheese,
   room temperature
1 tsp vanilla extract
450 g/1 lb icing sugar, sifted

1. Preheat the oven to 170°C/ 325°F/ Gas 3. Line a 12-hole non-stick muffin tin with paper cases.

2. Whisk the egg yolks and milk together in a bowl. In a separate bowl, whisk together the oil and sugar and add this to the egg mixture.

3. Sift the flour and baking powder and add to the batter, mixing thoroughly. Add the beetroot, hazelnuts and cinnamon, and stir to combine.

4. In a large clean bowl, whisk the egg whites until they form stiff peaks. Using a metal spoon, gently fold the whites into the pink batter. Keep turning the mixture so that the two are combined.

5. Divide the mixture between the paper cases. Bake in the centre of the preheated oven for 20 minutes. Remove and place the cakes on a wire rack to cool.

6. Whisk the butter and cream cheese together, then add the vanilla extract. Stir in the icing sugar a third at a time, making sure it is well mixed in. Pipe the icing onto the cakes or spread it onto them with a palette knife.

Spooky ghost cakes

These need to be baked in special dariole moulds (pudding-shaped moulds), but I think they are worth the investment, especially if you make them every year. The cakes are super-quick to make and topped with delicious meringue icing. *Makes 8.*

2 tbsp sunflower oil, plus extra
   for greasing
170 g/6 oz self-raising flour
½ tsp baking powder
75 g/2½ oz caster sugar
150 ml/5 fl oz milk
1 medium egg

For the meringue icing
170 g/6 oz caster sugar
1 large egg white
2 tbsp hot water
pinch of cream of tartar
16 currants, lightly flattened

1. Preheat the oven to 180°C/ 350°F/Gas 4. Grease 8 dariole moulds lightly – I put a little sunflower oil on some kitchen paper and gently wipe them with that. Cut 8 small circles of greaseproof paper to fit in the base of each mould so the cakes come out easily.

2. Sift the flour, baking powder and sugar into a bowl. Gently whisk together the milk, egg and sunflower oil and pour over the dry ingredients, mixing to get rid of any lumps.

3. Pour the mixture into the moulds so they are almost full, then place them on a baking sheet and bake in the centre of the oven for 15–20 minutes. Check that the tops of the cakes feel firm and a skewer inserted comes out clean, then remove to a wire rack to cool.

4. Gently ease the cakes out of the moulds and turn them upside down so their narrowest point is at the top. You may have to trim off a little at the base to ensure that they stand up.

5. To make the icing, put all the ingredients in a heatproof bowl and set it over a pan of simmering water. Beat with an electric whisk until soft peaks begin to form as you lift the whisk – this will take 5–6 minutes.

6. Working quickly, top the cakes with the icing. Spoon about a tablespoon onto each one, then use a palette knife to ease the icing down until it covers the whole cake. Do this on the serving plate, as a little frosting will puddle at the base of each cake. Use the flattened currants to create hollow ghostly eyes.

Bonfire cupcakes

These look wonderfully dramatic, and although it may seem extravagant to use four boxes of Matchmakers, the wow factor will be worth it. The easiest way to deal with these is to eat the Matchmakers before moving on to the cake. *Makes 12.*

½ tbsp lemon juice or vinegar
110 ml/4 fl oz full-fat milk
110 g/4 oz plain flour
½ tsp bicarbonate of soda
25 g/1 oz cocoa powder
55 g/2 oz unsalted butter,
    room temperature
125 g/4½ oz caster sugar
1 large egg

For the icing
110 g/4 oz unsalted butter,
    room temperature
110 g/4 oz cream cheese,
    room temperature
450 g/1 lb icing sugar
1 tsp vanilla essence
1 tsp red food colouring paste
4 packets of Matchmakers

1. Preheat the oven to 180°C/ 350°F/Gas 4. Line a 12-hole non-stick muffin tin with paper cake cases. Add the lemon juice or vinegar to the milk and set it to one side to allow the milk to curdle. Sift the flour, bicarbonate and cocoa in a bowl and set aside.

2. Cream the butter and half the sugar together in a large bowl until pale and creamy. Add the egg, followed by the rest of the sugar. Follow this with a third of the cocoa mixture, then a third of the soured milk; keep alternating until you have used up all the mixtures.

3. Divide the mixture between the cases. Place in the oven and bake for 20–25 minutes until firm and springy to the touch. Remove to a wire rack and leave to cool.

4. Beat together the butter and cream cheese for the icing until smooth. Add the icing sugar a third at a time and continue to mix, adding the vanilla and then the red food colouring to achieve a strong red colour.

5. Turn the cupcakes upside down and remove their paper cases. Using a butter knife or spatula, cover the cakes (still upside down) in red icing. Build up the icing on the cakes and create high peaks.

6. While the icing is still soft, press in the 'logs' (Matchmakers) which you can break to fit. Some should be higher than the cake and you can use the shorter pieces to fill in the gaps. The iced peak should show just over the top of the logs to give the impression of a flame.

Bloody hand cookies

ou will need to invest in a hand-shaped cookie cutter (see Suppliers, page 160) for these gloriously gory treats. This is great for getting the kids involved and they will just love the messy job of dripping the jam-blood strategically over the hands. *Makes 6–8.*

200 g/7 oz unsalted butter,
   room temperature
170 g/6 oz sugar
2 eggs
1 tsp vanilla extract

310 g/11 oz plain flour
1 tsp baking powder
½ tsp salt
6–8 tbsp raspberry jam

1. Preheat the oven to 200°C/400°F/Gas 6. You will need a large baking sheet.

2. Cream together the butter and sugar until light and fluffy. Add the eggs, one at a time, followed by the vanilla. Sift the flour, baking powder and salt into a separate bowl, then add to the butter mixture. Stir until thoroughly combined, but don't overmix.

3. Cover with clingfilm and place the mixture in the fridge to chill for at least an hour. I often leave mine overnight.

4. Remove the dough from the fridge and knead it lightly – you may find it easier to divide it into two first. Place the dough between two layers of greaseproof paper and use a rolling pin to roll it out to a thickness of about 1cm/½in. Remove the top sheet of greaseproof and use a hand cutter to stamp out shapes. If you have left and right hand cutters, do half of each. If you only have one, turn it upside down to do half the cookies so they match when sandwiched together.

5. Trim off any excess dough around the shapes and then pop the greaseproof paper with the hand shapes onto a baking sheet. Bake for 6–8 minutes until the cookies are turning golden at the edges. Remove from the oven and allow to cool.

6. Sandwich the hands together with generous dollops of raspberry jam so that it oozes out at the edges.

Spiced apple cookies

I first made these with fallen apples from the garden. They are packed full of flavour and heady with spice. *Makes about 24.*

60 ml/2 fl oz sunflower oil
75 g/2½ oz unsalted butter,
    room temperature
100 g/3½ oz demerara sugar
55 g/2 oz dark muscovado
    sugar
1 egg

1 tsp vanilla extract
100 g/3½ oz porridge oats
150 g/5½ oz rice flour
½ tsp baking powder
½ tsp bicarbonate of soda
1 tsp Chinese five-spice powder
150 g/5½ oz grated apple

1. Preheat the oven to 180°C/ 350°F/Gas 4. You will need a large ungreased baking sheet.

2. Mix together the oil, butter and sugars in a large bowl and beat until the mixture is smooth. Beat in the egg, followed by the vanilla, then stir in the oats.

3. Sift the flour, baking powder, bicarbonate and spice into another bowl. Using a wooden spoon, stir the flour into the oat and egg mixture. Add the grated apple and mix until combined.

4. Spoon tablespoons of the mixture onto the baking sheet. Leave about 5cm/2in between each one as the cookies will expand. Bake for 10 minutes until the surface is set. Allow the cookies to cool on the baking sheet for about 5 minutes, then transfer to a wire rack.

Chocolate toffee cookies

A winning combination – these won't stay around for long. My mum used to whip them up after we'd been out trick-or-treating to use up the glut of toffees and chocolate we'd return home with. *Makes 24.*

225 g/8 oz unsalted butter, room temperature
170 g/6 oz granulated sugar
170 g/6 oz soft light brown sugar
2 large eggs
1 tsp vanilla extract

400 g/13 oz plain flour
1 tsp bicarbonate of soda
½ tsp baking powder
225 g/8 oz milk chocolate, chopped
170 g/6 oz toffees, chopped

1. Preheat the oven to 170°C/ 325°F/Gas 3. You will need a large baking sheet.

2. Begin by beating the butter and sugars together until light and fluffy. Add the eggs, mixing them in one by one, and the vanilla.

3. Sift the flour with the bicarbonate and baking powder, and beat into the mixture. Add the chocolate and toffee.

4. Drop tablespoonfuls of mixture onto an ungreased baking sheet. Leave 5cm/2in between them. Bake for 10–12 minutes, then remove and cool on a wire rack.

Pumpkin marshmallow cookies

These have an almost cake-like texture. I adapted them from a recipe my friend sent from America and added my own twist with the marshmallow filling. *Makes 16–20 (8–10 sandwiches).*

225 g/8 oz unsalted butter,
  room temperature
225 g/8 oz caster sugar
225 g/8 oz canned pumpkin
  purée
1 egg
225 g/8 oz plain flour
1 tsp baking powder
1 tsp cinnamon

½ tsp nutmeg
½ tsp salt

For the filling
170 g/6 oz caster sugar
1 egg white
2 tbsp hot water
pinch of cream of tartar

1. Preheat the oven to 190°C/ 375°F/Gas 5. You will also need a large ungreased baking sheet.

2. Cream together the butter and sugar and add the pumpkin purée.

3. Next add the egg and mix well. Mix the dry ingredients together, and combine with the creamed mixture.

4. Drop spoonfuls of batter onto the baking sheet, leaving about 5cm/2in between them. Bake in the preheated oven for 12–14 minutes. Remove and cool on the baking sheet.

5. Meanwhile, make the filling. Place all the ingredients in a heatproof bowl and place over a pan of hot (not boiling) water. Use an electric whisk to beat the mixture until it thickens and forms soft peaks when you lift the whisk. Remove the bowl from the heat.

6. When the cookies are cool, spread filling on half of them and top these with the rest of the cookies to make sandwiches.

Fruit and nut cookies

e like to wrap a couple of these in brown paper to slip in our pockets before trekking through the fields surrounding Shimpling, our country home. This works a treat in winter when we take them straight from the oven and use them as make-shift hand warmers. *Makes three or four dozen, depending on size.*

170 g/6 oz unsalted butter,
   room temperature
170 g/6 oz brown sugar
85 g/3 oz caster sugar
1 egg
2 tsp vanilla extract
2 tbsp water
110 g/4 oz wholemeal flour

½ tsp salt
1 tsp bicarbonate of soda
1 tsp ground cinnamon
225 g/8 oz porridge oats
170 g/6 oz sultanas
85 g/3 oz walnuts
85 g/3 oz hazelnuts

1. Preheat the oven to 180°C/350°F/ Gas 4. You will need a large baking sheet.

2. Use an electric mixer to beat the butter and sugars together, until paler in colour and creamy. Add the egg with the vanilla and water.

3. Sift together the flour, salt, bicarbonate and the cinnamon and add to the butter mixture. Then add the oats, sultanas and nuts.

4. Roll the mixture into balls about the size of a golfball in your hands and then flatten slightly. Place them about 5cm/2in apart on an ungreased baking sheet. Bake in the centre of the oven for 15 minutes so that the edges are crispy but the centre is still soft.

5. Remove from the oven and leave to cool for 3 or 4 minutes on the baking sheet before gently transferring to a cooling rack.

Maple pecan cookies

One of my all-time favourite combinations and one that seems particularly perfect at this time of year. *Makes 24.*

110 g/4 oz unsalted butter, room temperature
255 g/9 oz granulated sugar
85 g/3 oz dark brown sugar
1 egg

½ tsp vanilla extract
285 g/10 oz plain flour
1 tsp bicarbonate of soda
2 tbsp maple syrup
55 g/2 oz pecans, chopped

1. Preheat the oven to 150°C/ 300°F/Gas 2. Grease 2 baking sheets.

2. Using an electric mixer (or a wooden spoon), beat the butter and sugars together until light and fluffy. Add the egg and vanilla.

3. Sift over the flour and bicarbonate, and stir to blend. Add the maple syrup and the nuts and mix well.

4. Drop heaped tablespoons of the mixture onto the prepared baking sheets. Bake for 8–10 minutes until lightly golden. Remove to a wire rack with a spatula and leave to cool.

Peanut butter dips

The contrast of the slight saltiness of the crumbly peanut butter with the sweet chocolate is what makes these so moreish. I love making these with my nieces and nephew. Needless to say, most of the chocolate seems to end up on their hands and faces instead of on the cookies! *Makes 20.*

110 g/4 oz unsalted butter, room temperature
225 g/8 oz demerara sugar
1 medium egg
4 tbsp crunchy peanut butter

200 g/7 oz plain flour
1 tsp baking powder
110 g/4 oz plain chocolate, for dipping

1. Preheat the oven to 180°C/350°F/Gas 4. You will need a large baking sheet.

2. Cream the butter and sugar together until light and fluffy. Add the egg, stir in the peanut butter and then the flour and baking powder.

3. Roll the mixture into balls the size of large walnuts and place them 5cm/2in apart on a baking sheet. Bake for 12 minutes in the preheated oven. The cookies will look like they are not cooked, but don't worry – they will carry on cooking as they cool.

4. While the cookies are in the oven, melt the chocolate in a bowl over a pan of simmering water or in the microwave for 90 seconds. Using a palette knife, spread one side of the cookies with chocolate and place them on a wire rack to set.

Winter

...chocolate kisses,
snowdrifts and shortbread...

Snow falls silently, drenching the drive and icing the trees and hills as far as the eye can see. To me the scene means one thing – Christmas is on its way and it is by far my favourite time of year. I love the build-up, the making of presents, cards and wrapping paper. I love the hand-made decorations we add to each year. The various kinds mark different phases in our lives: bright-feathered birds, wool-haired angels, moulded stars and moons painted silver and gold all play their role in decorating the tree, but must jostle for space with the make-shift, fleeting decorations that are added to the emerald branches last. These are gingered biscuits decorated with red and white rustic patterns, turning lazily on gold thread, their spicy scent mingling with the trace of forest pine.

What I savour most is the food we'll eat – the delicious Christmas-themed bites of nostalgia and tradition, as well as new flavours that encapsulate all that Christmas means. My favourite part of the preparations is making the sweet treats to delight my family. There is nothing that pleases me more than seeing the table laden with exquisite fancies and groaning under the weight of these extraordinary delicacies. I pull out the ancient ruby-red tablecloth and throw it over the table, ready for the plates piled high with my finest creations. I begin with the White Christmas cupcakes, their creamy macadamias nestled in a citrusy sponge and hidden beneath a pale frosting smattered with coconut. Next to them I place the Christmas pudding cupcakes, their dense fruitiness set off by a booze-soaked almond butter icing. The room is filling with a complex aroma of fruits and spices, but now there are heady chocolate overtones as the chocolate orange cookies arrive, still warm from the oven. Then come the deeply satisfying Christmas cakes, full of aromatic spices, studded with delicate shards of almond and walnut and bathed in a cloak of snow-white icing that is crisp to the bite. Hand-baked, fabulously rich baroque and snowdrift shortbread complete the spread – a delectable combination of biscuit, toffee, chocolate, pecans, cranberries and silver and gold baubles. These are best cut into tiny pieces and handed round while indulging in some glorious movie, savouring the warm feelings that come from communing with your loved ones – despite no one uttering a word.

But for us the day must begin with the luscious taste of Christmas breakfast buns, a fittingly extravagant way to begin the day. These are greedily devoured as we open our stockings. The voluptuous buns are filled with chopped pecans sitting in a golden paste of cinnamon butter and brown sugar that is still bubbling on top. I can't help but take another, even though I know I should pace myself with so much more feasting ahead. As I bite into the spicy bun my mind drifts back...

The fire-engine-red Aga is at full pelt and both the open fires are blazing, trying desperately to take the edge of the frozen air in this rambling home. I perch gingerly on the edge of the old range, which is dangerous for two reasons: one, I may burn my bottom, and two, I may be told off. I don't really see the point of the telling-off, though, as I have already dented both shiny silver tops. (It's not as if I can do any more harm, is it?) Mum realizes this and shows it with her half-hearted admonishments.

This is the warmest spot in the house, apart from the narrow niche between the dresser and the Aga, but I am growing by the day and beginning to feel the squeeze. I chatter away to Mum as she mixes with the wooden spoon and opens and closes each oven door. She seems to be juggling a dozen dishes, balancing them precariously and uttering the occasional curse as the threadbare Royal Wedding tea towel fails to protect her hand. She is weighing and stirring and mixing. I am transfixed, for I know that when popped in the oven this crude batter will perform all kinds of acrobatics, puff up with pride at what it has become and develop a texture of delicate sponge. I can barely contain myself, waiting for the moment when the oven door is flung open and I am enveloped in a cocoon of sticky, rich scent. The almond-vanilla smell is so heady that it is already on my tongue, tickling my taste buds and tantalizing my mouth to involuntary watering.

At last the battered tin is lifted majestically from the mouth of the Aga and placed next to me, where I gaze longingly. The moment Mum turns her back to find a wire rack I lean over and steal a cake. I quickly take a bite, knowing that by then it is too late for anything to be done about it. When she looks round it is already half devoured – the heat of the cake making the texture dense and cloying, but in a very good way. My eyes have closed as I savour the taste and Mum surprises me as I hear her honeyed voice agreeing – they do taste best straight from the oven. I put the rest of the cake to one side and lean into her, throwing my arms around her neck, smelling that most familiar smell, as her hair falls heavy over me.

White Christmas cupcakes

I wanted to come up with a cupcake with a real Christmassy flavour, something that would appeal to the younger members of the family who often aren't keen on dried fruit and spice. I can think of no more festive flavour than the bright orange clementine. These orangey cupcakes with snowy white chocolate and macadamias, topped off with coconut shavings, have great appeal for one and all. *Makes 12.*

110 g/4 oz unsalted butter,
   room temperature
110 g/4 oz sugar
2 eggs
140 g/5 oz self-raising flour
1 tsp baking powder
55 g/2 oz macadamia nuts
85 g/3 oz white chocolate
zest of 3 clementines
juice of 1 clementine

For the meringue icing
170 g/6 oz caster sugar
1 large egg white
2 tbsp hot water
pinch of cream of tartar
desiccated coconut,
   to decorate

1. Preheat the oven to 180°C/ 350°F/Gas 4. Line a 12-hole non-stick muffin tin with paper muffin cases.

2. Cream the butter and sugar together until pale and fluffy. Add the eggs one at a time, beating well. Sift the flour and baking powder together and add this a third at a time to the batter. Chop the macadamia nuts and the white chocolate and add them to the mixture with the clementine zest and juice.

3. Spoon the mixture into the paper cases so that they are three-quarters full. Bake the cakes in the centre of the preheated oven for about 20 minutes. Check with a skewer – if the cakes are cooked the skewer should come out clean. Remove from the oven and place the cakes on a wire rack to cool.

4. Put all the icing ingredients, except the coconut, into a heatproof bowl over a pan of simmering water. Beat with an electric whisk until soft peaks begin to form as you lift the whisk.

5. Working quickly, ice the cooled cakes, forming swirls with a palette knife. Sprinkle with desiccated coconut and leave to set.

Ginger pudding cakes

I just had to make something that looked like a traditional Christmas Pudding and this was what I came up with. These are also delicious served with a traditional rum sauce. *Makes 24.*

170 g/6 oz golden syrup
170 g/6 oz black treacle
170 g/6 oz unsalted butter
255 g/9 oz caster sugar
255 g/9 oz plain flour
1 tsp bicarbonate of soda
1 tsp ginger
1 tsp mixed spice
2 medium eggs
120 ml/4 fl oz boiling water

For the icing
255 g/8 oz fondant icing sugar
silver balls or holly and berry
  sprinkles, to decorate

1. Preheat the oven to 170°C/ 325°F/Gas 3. Line two 12-hole non-stick muffin tins with paper cases.

2. Heat the syrup, treacle, butter and sugar together in a heavy-based pan and gently bring them to the boil.

3. Sift the flour, bicarbonate and spices, then slowly stir them into the syrup mixture and mix until all the ingredients are incorporated. Remove from the heat and allow to cool for a few minutes. Add the eggs and beat well, then stir in the water.

4. Divide the mixture between the cake cases and bake in the centre of the oven for 18–20 minutes or until a skewer inserted comes out clean.

Use a knife to loosen the cakes by running it between the edge of the cake and the tin. Once all the cakes have been loosened, place the tin upside down on a wire rack to release the cakes. Leave to cool.

5. Sift the icing sugar into a medium-sized bowl and add 3 tablespoons of cold water. Beat with an electric whisk. If the icing looks too thick to spread, add another tablespoon of water.

6. Turn the cakes upside down so that they resemble Christmas puddings and spoon the icing onto the top of each of them. It should be just the right consistency to start falling down the sides. Finish each one with silver balls or holly and berry sprinkles.

Christmas spice cupcakes

I wanted to come up with a cupcake with a real Christmassy flavour. These cakes have all the spicy headiness that we associate with fruitcake but none of the heaviness. *Makes 12 large cupcakes.*

3 medium eggs, separated
55 g/2 oz caster sugar
70 ml/2½ fl oz vegetable oil
60 ml/2 fl oz water
1 tbsp honey
100 g/3½ oz muscovado sugar
75 g/2½ oz plain flour
1 tsp baking powder
½ tsp bicarbonate of soda
45 g/1½ oz ground almonds

1 tsp ground cinnamon
1 tsp ground ginger
1 tsp allspice
zest of 2 clementines

For the meringue icing
1 large egg white
170 g/6 oz caster sugar
silver balls, to decorate

1. Preheat the oven to 180°C/ 350°F/Gas 4. Line a 12-hole non-stick muffin tin with paper cases.

2. Whisk the egg whites so that they are beginning to stiffen into peaks, then add the caster sugar and continue whisking for a couple of minutes. Set aside.

3. Whisk the egg yolks with the oil and water and add the honey and muscovado sugar. Sift the flour with the baking powder and bicarbonate and fold gently into the egg mixture with the ground almonds, spices and zest. Using a metal spoon, fold the egg whites into the mixture until just combined.

4. Spoon the mixture into the paper cases. Bake in the centre of the oven for 20–25 minutes until the cakes are springy to the touch. Remove and place on a wire rack to cool.

5. To make the icing, place the egg white in a heatproof bowl over a pan of simmering water. Use an electric whisk to beat the egg white until it begins to stiffen. Add 30 g/1 oz of the sugar and beat for a minute before adding another 30 g/1 oz and beating for another minute. Continue until all the sugar is used up. Whisk for 4–6 minutes until the mixture is glossy and has doubled in size.

6. Once the cakes have cooled, coat each one with a tablespoon of the icing. Use a palette knife to smooth over the top of the cake. Sprinkle with silver balls.

Christmas pudding cupcakes

My mum insisted that I include this recipe for the sake of tradition. I wasn't too sure, until I had the inspired idea of adapting my grandma's brandy butter recipe into a buttercream icing. This sets the cakes off beautifully. *Makes 24.*

200 g/7 oz sultanas
140 g/5 oz currants
6 dates, stoned and chopped
170 g/6 oz unsalted butter,
    room temperature
255 g/9 oz dark muscovado
    sugar
3 large eggs
170 g/6 oz self-raising flour
1 medium apple, peeled and
    grated

½ tsp mixed spice
4 tbsp rum

For the icing
140 g/5 oz unsalted butter,
    room temperature
225 g/8 oz icing sugar, sifted
55 g/2 oz ground almonds
3 tbsp brandy
holly and berry sprinkles,
    to decorate

1. Preheat the oven to 170°C/325°F/ Gas 3. Line two 12-hole non-stick muffin tins with paper cases.

2. Place the sultanas, currants and dates in a pan. Cover with water and bring to the boil. Turn the heat down and simmer for 15 minutes so the fruits are soft and swollen.

3. Beat the butter and sugar together until the colour begins to lighten. Add the eggs, one at a time, followed by the flour. Stir in the grated apple, spice, rum, and the drained fruit.

4. Divide the mixture between the paper cases. Bake in the centre of the preheated oven for 25 minutes. Insert a skewer or knife in the centre to check that the mixture is cooked. Remove and turn the cakes out onto a wire rack to cool.

5. Make the icing. Using an electric whisk, cream the butter so that it is soft. Start adding the icing sugar a third at a time and keep beating until the mixture is pale and creamy. Add the ground almonds, beat again, and after a minute add the brandy a tablespoon at a time. Check the flavour and adjust to taste.

6. Spoon the mixture into an icing bag with a plain nozzle. Pipe onto the cooled cakes, beginning from the outside and working towards the centre in a circular motion. Sprinkle with holly and berry decorations.

Chocolate devil's food cupcakes

These wicked cakes are one of my favourites – as the name suggests, they are positively naughty, chocolatey, delectable and incredibly indulgent. *Makes 12.*

½ tbsp lemon juice or vinegar
110 ml/4 fl oz full-fat milk
110 g/4 oz plain flour
½ tsp bicarbonate of soda
25 g/1 oz cocoa powder
55 g/2 oz unsalted butter,
    room temperature
125 g/4½ oz caster sugar
1 large egg

For the icing
125 g/4½ oz plain chocolate,
    broken into pieces
small pinch of salt
1½ tbsp caster sugar
150 ml/5 fl oz soured cream
gold chocolate buttons,
    to decorate

1. Preheat the oven to 180°C/350°F/Gas 4. Line a 12-hole non-stick muffin tin with paper muffin cases.

2. Add the lemon juice or vinegar to the milk and set aside.

3. Sift the flour, bicarbonate and cocoa into a medium-sized bowl.

4. In a separate bowl, cream the butter and half the sugar together until light and fluffy. Then beat in the egg, followed by the remainder of the sugar. Beat in the flour and cocoa mixture, a third at a time, alternating with a third of the soured milk mixture, until everything is mixed in.

5. Spoon the mixture into the paper cases. Place in the centre of the oven and bake for 20–25 minutes until they are firm and springy to the touch, and a skewer inserted into the centre comes out clean. Remove from the oven and place the cakes on a wire rack to cool.

6. To make the icing, melt the chocolate in a heatproof bowl set over a pan of barely simmering water. Stir until the chocolate is melted. Whisk in the salt, sugar and soured cream and remove from the heat. Leave for 10 minutes to cool.

7. Using a palette knife, swirl the icing over the tops of the cakes. Top each one with a gold chocolate button.

Cinnamon banana cupcakes

These cakes are full of aphrodisiac ingredients, making them a perfect Valentine's Day gift. Walnuts are a stimulant, the banana is a symbol of fertility and it has been said that the Queen of Sheba used an attar made from cinnamon to seduce King Solomon. *Makes 12.*

110 g/4 oz unsalted butter,
room temperature
110 g/4 oz caster sugar
2 large eggs
1 egg yolk
140 g/5 oz self-raising flour
1 tsp baking powder
2 bananas, mashed
1 tsp cinnamon
55 g/2 oz chopped walnuts

For the icing
55 g/2 oz unsalted butter,
room temperature
pinch of salt
1 tsp vinegar
1 banana, mashed
300 g/10 oz icing sugar, sifted
¼ tsp cinnamon

1. Preheat the oven to 180°C/350°F/Gas 4. Line a 12-hole non-stick muffin tin with paper muffin cases.

2. Cream the butter and sugar until light and fluffy, then beat in the eggs, one at a time, and the egg yolk and mix well.

3. Sift the flour and baking powder together and add this, a third at a time, to the batter, followed by the mashed banana, cinnamon and the walnuts.

4. Spoon the mixture into the paper cases so that they are three-quarters full. Bake the cakes in the centre of the preheated oven for about 20 minutes until they are firm and springy to the touch and a skewer inserted into the centre comes out clean. Remove from the oven and place the cakes on a wire rack to cool.

5. To make the icing, cream the butter with the salt. Mix the vinegar into the mashed banana. Add the banana mixture to the butter a little at a time, alternating with the icing sugar, then add the cinnamon. Beat the icing until it is creamy.

6. Using a spatula, cover each cake with about a tablespoon of icing.

Sweet heart cupcakes

These heart-shaped cakes are easy to make and don't require a special tin – who would have thought that the humble marble could be an indispensable piece of baking equipment! *Makes 12.*

40 g/1½ oz ground almonds
½ tsp baking powder
110 g/4 oz self-raising flour
110 g/4 oz unsalted butter,
    room temperature
110 g/4 oz caster sugar
2 large eggs
1 tsp vanilla extract

For the icing
75 g/3 oz icing sugar, sifted
red food colouring paste

12 marbles or equivalent-sized
  pieces of tin foil

1. Preheat the oven to 180°C/ 350°F/Gas 4. Line a 12-hole non-stick muffin tin with paper muffin cases.

2. Sift the ground almonds, baking powder and flour into a medium-sized bowl.

3. In a separate bowl, cream together the butter and sugar until pale and fluffy. Then beat in the eggs, one at a time. Stir in the flour mixture until fully combined.

4. Spoon the mixture into the paper cases. Now tuck a marble into each hole in the tin, just between the case and the tin itself. This will create an indentation in the case which will result in a heart-shaped edge once the cakes are baked. Bake for 15–20 minutes until they are firm and springy to the touch, and a skewer inserted into the centre comes out clean. Remove from the oven and place the cakes on a wire rack to cool.

5. To make the icing, mix the icing sugar with enough water to achieve a consistency a little thicker than single cream. Add enough red colouring paste to make a bright shade of red. Pour or spread the icing over each cake using a spatula or palette knife.

Christmas breakfast buns

These are deliciously decadent for breakfast time but don't let that stop you having them any other time of the day or night. *Makes 12.*

110 g/4 oz unsalted butter,
  room temperature
110 g/4 oz golden caster sugar
3 eggs
225 g/8 oz plain flour
1 tsp bicarbonate of soda
1 tsp baking powder
300 ml/10 fl oz double cream

For the filling and topping
55 g/2 oz unsalted butter
170 g/6 oz soft dark brown
  sugar
2 tsp cinnamon
140 g/5 oz pecans, chopped

1. Preheat the oven to 170°C/325°F/Gas 3. Line a 12-hole non-stick muffin tin with large paper muffin cases.

2. First make the topping and filling mixture. Rub the butter into the dark brown sugar along with the cinnamon. Once the mixture has the texture of sand, stir in the nuts.

3. To make the bun batter, cream the butter and sugar together until pale and fluffy. Add the eggs, one at a time, beating for about 30 seconds between each one.

4. Sift the flour, bicarbonate and baking powder together in a medium-sized bowl. Add this to the butter mixture in two parts, alternating with the double cream.

5. Put a tablespoon of the batter into each paper case, making sure you cover the base right up to the edges. With a teaspoon, create an indent in the middle of the cake, but make sure there is still a couple of centimetres of batter below it. Use a scant teaspoon of the pecan sugar mixture to fill the hole, then cover with a tablespoon of batter making sure to cover the sugar. Top with another teaspoon of the pecan sugar mixture.

6. Bake in the centre of the oven for 20–25 minutes. The buns should rise up a little over the edges of the cases and the sugar on top should bubble up. Remove and place on a wire rack to cool for about 5 minutes. Eat while still warm.

Christmas spice biscuits

These are satisfying to make and have a simple rustic beauty when strung on ribbon and hung on the Christmas tree. Their spicy aroma fills the room and if you hang some out of reach, tiny people won't be able to plough through them too quickly. *Makes about 40.*

340 g/12 oz plain flour
1 tsp bicarbonate of soda
1 tsp ginger
2 tsp cinnamon
110 g/4 oz unsalted butter,
  room temperature
70 g/6 oz light muscovado
  sugar
1 egg, beaten
4 tbsp golden syrup

For the icing
2 egg whites
285–400 g/10–14 oz icing
  sugar, sifted
¼–½ tsp red food colouring
  paste
silver balls, to decorate

1. Preheat the oven to 170°C/ 325°F/Gas 3. You will need a large greased baking sheet.

2. Sift the flour with the bicarbonate, ginger and cinnamon. Cream the butter and sugar together until pale and fluffy and add the egg and golden syrup. Mix well, then add the flour mixture and mix again until a firm dough is formed.

3. Sprinkle a little flour onto your worksurface. Roll out the mixture to about 1 cm thick. Cut into rounds with a 4cm/1½in cutter, then gather the offcuts to re-roll and cut more biscuits.

4. Place the cookies on the baking sheet, leaving space between them as they will spread. Use a skewer to make a hole near the edge of the biscuits so you can thread a ribbon through and hang them on the tree. Bake for 8–10 minutes, then place on a wire rack to cool.

5. Put the egg whites in a bowl and stir in the icing sugar a little at a time. Keep stirring and adding until you have a fairly firm consistency. Remove half the icing to a separate bowl, stir in the red colouring paste and set aside.

6. Spoon the icing into two separate piping bags and decorate the cooled biscuits with stars, hearts and circles. Add a few silver balls. Allow to dry before threading through with ribbon and hanging on the tree.

Chocolate orange cookies

I suggest that you buy extra chocolate oranges for this recipe, as in my experience people can be rather territorial with their own. *Makes 30.*

200 g/7 oz plain flour, unsifted
55 g/2 oz cocoa powder
1 tsp bicarbonate of soda
1–2 tsp salt
110 g/4 oz unsalted butter,
    room temperature
255 g/9 oz granulated sugar
55 g/2 oz soft brown sugar

2 eggs, lightly beaten
1 tsp vanilla extract
2 tbsp Cointreau
1 tbsp grated orange zest
225 g/8 oz chocolate (use
    chocolate orange if you have
    some), chopped into pieces

1. Preheat the oven to 170°C/ 325°F/Gas 3. You will need a large ungreased baking sheet.

2. Mix the flour, cocoa powder, bicarbonate and salt together. In a separate bowl, cream the butter and sugars until fluffy, then add the eggs, one at a time, followed by the vanilla, Cointreau and zest. Beat until creamy. Mix in the flour and stir until combined, then stir in the chocolate pieces.

3. Drop rounded tablespoons of the mixture onto the baking sheet. Bake in the preheated oven for 10–12 minutes until just golden and cool on a wire rack.

Baroque shortbread

A version of millionaire's shortbread, but this one is even richer and more decadent. A minor warning, the silver and gold balls can be hard on the teeth. *Makes 12 large pieces or 24 bite-sized.*

For the base
85 g/3 oz caster sugar
225 g/8 oz plain flour
110 g/4 oz unsalted butter,
    fridge cold

For the fudge filling
1 x 397 g can condensed milk
55 g/2 oz light muscovado
    sugar
55 g/2 oz unsalted butter

For the topping
55 g/2 oz pecans
85 g/3 oz plain chocolate
85 g/3 oz milk chocolate
15 g/½ oz unsalted butter
cranberries, to decorate
gold or silver balls,
    to decorate

1. Preheat the oven to 170°C/325°F/ Gas 3. You will need a greased baking tin measuring 20 x 30cm/8 x 12in.

2. In a large bowl, mix the sugar and flour together and add the butter. Rub the butter into the flour until the mixture resembles breadcrumbs.

3. Put the mixture into the baking tin and spread it evenly, pressing it firmly into the corners. Bake in the oven for 25 minutes until golden brown in colour. Remove and increase the oven temperature to 200°C/400°F/Gas 6.

4. While the base is baking, make the fudge filling. Pour the condensed milk into a pan, add the sugar and butter, and bring to the boil. Cook for 2–3

minutes, stirring constantly to make sure it doesn't burn. Take off the heat and set aside.

5. Place the pecans on a baking sheet and bake for 6 minutes. Don't let them burn. Melt the chocolate and butter in a bowl over a pan of simmering water, or put in a microwave for 90 seconds. Lightly mix the two chocolates to achieve a marbled effect.

6. Cover the shortbread with the fudge filling, top with the melted chocolate and leave to cool a little. Decorate with the pecans, some cranberries and gold and silver balls, cut into small squares and serve.

Snowdrift shortbread

Millionaire's shortbread has always been a weakness of mine and it occurred to me some years ago that it was the perfect Christmas treat, being somewhere between shortbread, toffees and chocolates. I think there is a simple elegance about this version which I created for my mum – there is nothing she likes as much as white chocolate. *Makes 12 large or 24 bite-sized.*

For the base
85 g/3 oz caster sugar
225 g/8 oz plain flour
110 g/4 oz unsalted butter, fridge-cold and cut into pieces

For the filling
1 x 397 g can condensed milk
55 g/2 oz soft light brown sugar
55 g/2 oz unsalted butter

For the topping
170 g/6 oz white Belgian chocolate
55 g/2 oz desiccated coconut

1. Preheat the oven to 170°C/325°F/ Gas 3. You will need a greased baking tin measuring 20 x 30cm/8 x 12in.

2. In a large bowl, mix the sugar and flour together and add the butter. Rub the butter into the flour until the mixture has the texture of breadcrumbs.

3. Put the dough into the baking tin and spread it evenly, pressing it firmly into the corners. Bake in the oven for 25 minutes until golden brown in colour.

4. Meanwhile, make the fudge filling. Pour the condensed milk into a medium-sized pan and add the sugar and butter. Bring to the boil and, stirring constantly, cook for 2–3 minutes, then set aside.

5. To make the topping, melt the chocolate in a bowl over a pan of simmering water or in a microwave for 90 seconds.

6. Once the shortbread is cooked, cover with the fudge filling, then spread on the melted chocolate. Add a sprinkling of desiccated coconut and leave to cool. Cut into small squares and serve.

Lavender heart cookies

An old-fashioned shortbread, subtly scented with lavender, makes a romantic Valentine's gift. *Makes 18.*

110 g/4 oz unsalted butter
55 g/2 oz caster sugar
170 g/6 oz plain flour
2 tbsp fresh lavender florets

or 1 tbsp dried culinary
lavender, roughly chopped
2 tbsp icing sugar for
sprinkling (optional)

1. Preheat the oven to 200°C/400°F/Gas 6. You will need a large greased baking sheet.

2. Cream together the butter and sugar until pale and fluffy. Stir in the flour and lavender and bring together in a soft ball. Cover and chill for 15 minutes.

3. Roll out the dough on a lightly floured surface. Using a 5cm/2in heart-shaped cutter, stamp out 18 biscuits. Place on a heavy baking sheet and bake for about 10 minutes, so they are just golden.

4. Leave the biscuits on the baking sheet for 5 minutes to set, then use a spatula to transfer them to a wire rack to cool. Drench with the icing sugar before serving, if you like.

Chocolate kisses

 really intense chocolate hit shrouded in a layer of icing sugar, these look cute in a pretty box. *Makes 24.*

170 g/6 oz plain chocolate
110 g/4 oz unsalted butter,
   room temperature,
   plus extra for greasing

110 g/4 oz caster sugar
2 eggs
255 g/9 oz plain flour
icing sugar, for dusting

1. Preheat the oven to 190°C/ 375°F/Gas 5. Grease two baking sheets with butter.

2. Melt the plain chocolate, either in the microwave or over a bowl of simmering water (don't allow it to boil). Stir the chocolate until it is melted. Leave to cool.

3. Cream together the butter and sugar until pale and fluffy, then add the eggs one by one. Sift the flour over this mixture and mix together.

4. Add this mixture to the chocolate and mix thoroughly until the chocolate dough is fully blended. Knead with your knuckles so that the dough is smooth, then wrap in clingfilm and chill for about an hour.

5. Remove the dough from the fridge and roll teaspoon-sized balls between your palms. Place the balls on the baking sheets and bake for 10–12 minutes. Dust with icing sugar and place on a wire rack to cool.

6. Once the chocolate kisses are cool, place them in a cellophane bag, tie with ribbon and a pretty gift tag, and present to your loved one.

Parties

...and Margarita and the
White Russian lived happily ever after...

The twinkling fairy lights glitter among the leaves in the garden like so many earth-bound stars. They throw a delicate light on the lawn, which is transformed into a magical fairy dwelling. Fairies swoop, hover and tiptoe, twisting and pirouetting to entertain one another. They are dressed in shimmering shades of lilac, sky blue and palest pink, with wings as fine as gossamer and wands that glint and glimmer in the twilight. I watch this beautiful sight for a while and then one diminutive creature creeps up to me and tugs on my dress. I swoop down and scoop her into my arms where I hold her close, despite the wriggling. I press my face against the top of her head to inhale that most exquisite smell of my own little girl. 'We are ready for cake now,' she says. It is a demand, not a suggestion.

Gently setting her down I smile to myself, as I step back into the kitchen. There before me is the beautiful Fairy Cake that I have spent the day making. Her wings are made of rice paper, which glows impressively when I light the candles, and all around her are little butterfly cakes that shimmer as they bathe in the glow of her light. When I carry my creation outside, the chattering voices are hushed, mouths fall open as they watch, mesmerised. In the flickering candlelight even I believe my cake has come to life. I lead the singing of the familiar tune with the little high voices accompanying me. When we come to the end, Kitty takes an enormous breath and blows out all four candles. The cake is just a cake again. The glistening pink icing is delicious and the raspberry jam with the chocolate cake is scrumptious. I rest on the garden bench as I lick my sticky fingers clean and take a short break. Soon there will be party bags to hand out and parents to greet, but not before the sweetie scramble.

I remember the sweetie scrambles we had when I was a small child on an island far away, where the lush green grass was always soaked in sunlight and I spent the happiest years of my childhood. There were no flat plains; all around, the land curved up and down, making hills that just asked to be rolled down. When we had parties there was always a sweetie scramble. Sometimes they would be dropped from a helicopter and it would seem as if the skies had opened, but instead of water raining down on us there were great splashes of sweets in myriad colours and flavours. We would run and leap and hold out our skirts to carry them. Children would stuff their pockets full and I once saw a child filling up an umbrella.

When preparing for parties, my sister and I would be commandeered to help with the Lamingtons. She would carefully dip the delicate sponge in the chocolate icing and I would roll it in the coconut. We were quite expert with chocolate Rice Krispie cakes, stirring the gloopy treacle with the molten chocolate and liquid gold butter, but the treacle, no matter how careful we were, would always cascade down the side of the green and gold tin and pool into the edge filling up the rim. (A sneaky little tongue would mop up the sweet nectar.) Brightly coloured balloons would be suspended from cotton wrapped around drawing pins stuck into the soft old beams of our house, and then we would hang reams of crepe paper cut into strips and twisted from wall to wall.

Now I live on a much bigger island and I have grown up – but not grown out of giving parties. For me, life is a continuous round of celebrations and the anticipation of them. I thrive on these occasions, on planning the theme, the costumes, and decorations, but most of all the cakes. I was so thrilled to think of cocktail cupcakes – a grown-up theme for something so much associated with childhood. The Margarita cupcakes were the first I made – that salt rim shocking the taste buds just in time to dazzle the tongue as it hits the tequila-lime-curd filling. The White Russian was a sophisticated flavour I came up with for my husband, as it's his favourite drink. It has a subtle creamy flavour that makes the perfect end to an evening…

The moon hangs low and heavy in the sky, lending a gentle glow to the faces of our guests, who are talking and dancing to a makeshift mariachi band. A gentle breeze flutters the deep-pink paper garlands that frame the garden, which is lit by chains of red chilli lights, twinkling amid the ivy draping the crumbling walls. The night is filled with promise.

I weave in and out of the revellers, smiling and chatting as my tray of cakes becomes lighter. My eyes scour the garden, looking for a glimpse of my love, for whom I have saved a single White Russian cupcake. My pace quickens, but a hand reaches over from behind me and grabs the cake. I feel a wave of disappointment; suddenly I am spun around and find myself thrown back across my lover's arm. He leans down to kiss me and I notice the precious cupcake safely enclosed in his hand.

Vanilla cupcakes

 perfect cupcake decorated with glistening bead-like sprinkles, this looks like it belongs in a jewellery box. *Makes 12.*

110 g/4 oz unsalted butter,
  room temperature
110 g/4 oz caster sugar
2 large eggs
110 g/4 oz self-raising flour
1 tsp baking powder
1 tsp vanilla extract

For the icing
225 g/8 oz unsalted butter,
  room temperature
340 g/12 oz icing sugar, sifted
2 tsp vanilla extract
sprinkles, to decorate

1. Preheat the oven to 180°C/ 350°F/Gas 4. Fill a 12-hole non-stick muffin tin with paper muffin cases.

2. Cream the butter and sugar together until pale and fluffy. Add the eggs, one at a time, beating well between each addition. Sift the flour and baking powder together and add this, a third at a time, to the batter, follow this with the vanilla extract.

3. Place in the centre of the oven and bake for about 20 minutes until the cakes are springy to the touch and a skewer inserted into the centre comes out clean. Place on a wire rack and leave to cool.

4. To make the icing, beat the butter until pale and creamy, then beat in the icing sugar and vanilla. Decorate as you please.

Red velvet cupcakes

A simple white swirl of pale icing is all that is needed to adorn these deep red vanilla cakes, shown on the front cover of this book. *Makes 12.*

140 g/5 oz plain flour
1½ tbsp cocoa powder
½ tsp bicarbonate of soda
½ tsp baking powder
pinch of salt
120 ml/4 fl oz buttermilk
1 tsp vinegar
½ tsp vanilla extract
½ tsp red food colouring
    paste
55 g/2 oz unsalted butter,
    room temperature

170 g/6 oz sugar
2 eggs

For the icing
110 g/4 oz unsalted butter,
    room temperature
110 g/4 oz cream cheese,
    room temperature
450 g/1 lb icing sugar, sifted
½ vanilla pod
1 tsp vanilla extract
coloured sprinkles,
    to decorate

1. Preheat the oven to 180°C/350°F/Gas 4. Line a 12-hole non-stick muffin tin with paper cases.

2. Sift the flour, cocoa powder, bicarbonate, baking powder (or cream of tartar), and salt into a medium bowl. In a separate bowl, whisk the buttermilk, vinegar, vanilla, and food colouring together until blended.

3. Cream the butter and sugar together until light and fluffy. Add the eggs, one at a time, beating well after each addition. Beat in the flour mixture, a third at a time, alternating with a third of the buttermilk mixture, until all is mixed in.

4. Divide the mixture between the paper cases. Bake in the centre of the preheated oven for 20 minutes until springy to the touch. Remove and turn the cakes out onto a wire rack to cool.

5. To make the icing, beat the butter and cheese until creamy. Add the icing sugar and beat until combined. Split the half vanilla pod and scrape out the seeds into the icing. Add the vanilla.

6. Spoon the icing into a piping bag with a star nozzle and ice the cupcakes, starting from the outside and working in towards the middle. Decorate with coloured sprinkles.

Jack Daniel's cupcakes

Jack Daniel's is my husband's favourite tipple, so I knew that I had to find a way to make it into a cupcake. The chocolate somehow intensifies the flavour. *Makes 24.*

200 g/7 oz plain flour
250 g/8½ oz golden caster
   sugar
½ tsp bicarbonate of soda
1 large egg
100 ml/3½ fl oz milk
30 g/1 oz yoghurt
1 tsp vanilla extract
110 g/4 oz unsalted butter
2 tbsp cocoa powder
2 tbsp Coca-Cola

For the icing
110 g/4 oz icing sugar
1 tbsp Coca-Cola
3 tbsp Jack Daniel's
½ tsp black extra food
   colouring paste
100 g/3½ oz dark chocolate
Cola bottle sweets,
   to decorate

1. Preheat the oven to 170°C/ 325°F/Gas 3. Line two 12-hole non-stick muffin tins with paper muffin cases.

2. Mix the flour, sugar and bicarbonate in a large bowl. Stir the egg with the milk, yoghurt and vanilla in a separate medium-sized bowl.

3. Gently melt the butter, cocoa and Coca-Cola in a medium-sized, heavy-based pan. Stir until all the ingredients are blended and then pour into the sugar and flour. Beat with a wooden spoon, then stir in the egg mixture.

4. Pour into the cake cases so they are two-thirds full and bake in the centre of the oven for 20–25 minutes until firm and springy to the touch. Leave to cool on a wire rack.

5. For the icing, sift the icing sugar and add the Coca-Cola and Jack Daniel's along with the food colouring. Melt the chocolate and stir it into the icing.

6. Working quickly before the icing starts to dry out, spread the icing over the cakes with a spatula. Decorate each one with a Cola jelly sweet.

White Russian cupcakes

 Elegantly flavoured, these are the perfect end to a meal. My husband thinks they are my best cupcakes. *Makes 12.*

110 g/4 oz unsalted butter,
    room temperature
110 g/4 oz caster sugar
2 eggs
110 g/4 oz self-raising flour
1 tsp baking powder
6 tbsp Kahlúa liqueur

For the icing
55 g/2 oz white chocolate
100 ml/3 fl oz sour cream
3 tsp Kahlúa liqueur
225 g/8 oz icing sugar, sifted
cocoa powder, for dusting

1. Preheat the oven to 180°C/350°F/Gas 4. Fill a 12-hole non-stick muffin tin with large paper muffin cases.

2. Cream the butter and sugar together until pale and fluffy. Beat in the eggs one at a time. Sift the flour and baking powder together and add this, a third at a time, to the batter. Add the Kahlúa.

3. Spoon the batter into the cake cases. Place in the centre of the oven and bake for about 20 minutes until they are springy to the touch and a skewer inserted into the centre comes out clean. Place on a wire rack and leave to cool.

4. Melt the chocolate in a bowl over a pan of simmering water. Add the sour cream and stir in the Kahlúa, followed by the icing sugar. Allow to cool a little until it is a spreading consistency. Ice the cakes and finish with a light dusting of cocoa powder.

Pina Colada cupcakes

To me, this is the ultimate cocktail as it was the first I ever had. The combination of moist pineapple interior and soft coconut frosting makes these cakes taste sensational and I like to adorn them with as many decorations as possible. I was particularly pleased with the monkey in the palm tree! *Makes 12.*

55 g/2 oz unsalted butter,
    room temperature
140 g/5 oz sugar
120 ml/4 fl oz coconut milk
1 large egg
140 g/5 oz plain flour
2 tsp baking powder
425 g/15 oz can of pineapple
    rings, drained and chopped
    small

For the icing
175 g/6 oz caster sugar
1 egg white
2 tbsp Malibu rum

1. Preheat the oven to 180°C/ 350°F/Gas 4. Line a 12-hole non-stick muffin tin with paper cases.

2. Cream the butter and the sugar together until light and fluffy. Mix the coconut milk and egg together and add to the butter and sugar; don't worry if it looks a little curdled at this stage.

3. Sift the flour with the baking powder and add to the mixture, followed by the chopped pineapple.

4. Divide the mixture between the paper cases and bake in the oven for 20 minutes until springy to the touch. Leave to cool on a wire rack.

5. Place the icing ingredients in a heatproof bowl and place over a bowl of hot (not boiling) water. Use an electric whisk to beat the mixture until it thickens and forms soft peaks when you lift the whisk. This should take 5–6 minutes. Remove the bowl from the heat and spread the icing on the cupcakes, working quickly before the icing sets. Decorate as you please.

Margarita cupcakes

I love that every note of the drink is hit with these cakes – first the tongue-tickling salt and the Triple Sec and lime frosting; then, as you take a bite of the sponge, your mouth is filled with a tequila-lime filling. Simply sublime. *Makes 12.*

110 g/4 oz unsalted butter,
   room temperature
110 g/4 oz sugar
2 large eggs
110 g/4 oz self-raising flour
1 tsp baking powder
3 tsp lemon essence

For the filling
85 g/3 oz butter
60 ml/2 fl oz fresh lime juice
2 large eggs
2 large egg yolks
110 g/4 oz caster sugar
grated zest of 2 limes
1–2 tbsp tequila

For the icing
110 g/4 oz unsalted butter,
   room temperature
110 g/4 oz cream cheese,
   room temperature
450 g/1 lb icing sugar, sifted
juice and grated zest of
   1 lime
1 tbsp Triple Sec
green food colouring paste
Maldon salt flakes,
   to decorate
grated lime zest, to decorate

1. Preheat the oven to 180°C/ 350°F/Gas 4. Fill a 12-hole non-stick muffin tin with paper cases.

2. Cream the butter and sugar together in a large bowl until fluffy. Add the eggs, and sift in the flour and baking powder; then add the lemon essence and mix until smooth.

3. Put a tablespoon of mixture into each cake case. Bake in the top part of the oven for 15–20 minutes until the tops feel springy and a skewer inserted comes out clean.

4. Meanwhile, prepare the filling. Heat the butter and lime juice in a pan over a medium heat until the butter melts. In a medium bowl, whisk the eggs, egg yolks and sugar together until blended. Continue whisking as you slowly incorporate the hot butter and lime mixture into the yolk mixture. Pour the mixture back into the pan and continue cooking over a medium heat. Keep stirring with a wooden spoon until it reaches boiling point and thickens – this should take about 5 minutes. Remove from the heat, strain into a bowl and add the lime

zest. Once the sauce has cooled, add the tequila to taste. Any unused filling can be stored in the freezer for up to 3 months.

5. To make the icing, beat the butter and cream cheese together in a large bowl. Add the icing sugar and mix well, then the lime juice and zest, Triple Sec and green food colouring to achieve the desired colour.

6. When the cakes are cool, remove their middles with a sharp knife or an apple corer and fill them with the lime filling. Using a palette knife, spread icing over the cakes. Complete the Margarita effect by sprinkling salt around the rim of each cupcake and a placing a little grated lime zest in the centre.

Bollywood cupcakes

These decadently decorated creations never fail to impress. Their vibrant clashing colours make them perfect for celebrations and the delicious spice-spiked carrot cake that lies within is nothing short of delicious. *Makes 12.*

110 g/4 oz plain flour
1 tsp baking powder
½ tsp salt
½ tsp cinnamon
½ tsp ground ginger
½ tsp mixed spice
2 large eggs
170 g/6 oz dark muscovado
  sugar
100 ml/3½ fl oz sunflower oil
2 carrots, peeled and grated
55 g/2 oz walnuts, chopped
55 g/2 oz sultanas

For the icing
110 g/4 oz unsalted butter,
  room temperature
110 g/4 oz cream cheese,
  room temperature
450 g/1 lb icing sugar
1 tsp vanilla extract
food colouring paste – red,
  orange, pink or purple
gold and silver decorations

1. Preheat the oven to 170°C/ 325°F/Gas 3. Line a 12-hole non-stick muffin tin with paper muffin cases.

2. Sift the flour, baking powder, salt and spices into a bowl and set aside. Whisk the eggs and sugar together in a large bowl until thick, then beat in the oil. Add the grated carrot, walnuts and sultanas and mix to combine, then gently stir in the flour mixture.

3. Divide the batter between the paper cases. Bake in the preheated oven for 30 minutes until the tops of the cakes are springy. Remove and

place the cakes on a wire rack to cool while you prepare the icing.

4. In a large bowl, whisk together the butter and cream cheese. Sift the icing sugar into the bowl and mix until smooth and light. Divide the icing into three and colour each with a strong Bollywood colour.

5. Using a piping bag with a large star tip, pipe from the outside of each cake, working inwards to cover. Try piping a ring in one colour around the edge and a different colour on the inside for contrast. Finish by sprinkling on some gold and silver balls or stars.

Banoffee cupcakes

I love turning classic desserts into cupcake recipes and this is one of my favourites. I just love the ooze of the caramel when you bite into the banana cake. You can now buy the caramel filling ready made, in which case you can skip the first step in this recipe. *Makes 12.*

110 g/4 oz unsalted butter, room temperature
110 g/4 oz soft brown sugar
2 large eggs
110 g/4 oz self-raising flour
1 ripe banana

For the toffee filling
1 x 397 g/14 oz can condensed milk (or ready-made caramel filling)

For the topping
400 ml/14 fl oz whipping cream
1 banana, sliced (optional)

1. If you are using condensed milk, first prepare the toffee filling; this needs to be done at least 3 hours in advance. Put the unopened can of condensed milk in a pan, cover with boiling water and boil for 3 hours. Keep the pan topped up with boiling water and do not let it boil dry.

2. After 3 hours, remove the pan from the heat and allow the can to cool. Once it is cool enough to handle, open and spoon out the toffee. This can be kept in a jar in the fridge for future use.

3. Preheat the oven to 180°C/ 350°F/Gas 4. Line a 12-hole non-stick muffin tin with paper cases.

4. Cream the butter and sugar together in a large bowl until light, pale and fluffy. Add the eggs, mixing them in one by one, then gently fold in the flour. Mash the banana and mix into the batter.

5. Divide the mixture between the paper cases and bake for 15–20 minutes. Remove when springy to the touch and place on a wire rack to cool.

6. Using a sharp knife or an apple corer, remove the centre of each cake and fill with the toffee. Whisk the cream to form soft peaks. Using a piping bag with a star nozzle, pipe cream on top of each cake. Decorate with banana slices, if you wish.

Chocolate malt cupcakes

These are the cakes that my granny used to make us. She would always turn a blind eye to the fact that the bag of Maltesers used to decorate them was half-eaten by the time she needed them! *Makes 24.*

225 g/8 oz unsalted butter
150 g/5 oz plain chocolate,
    85 per cent cocoa solids
4 large eggs
225 g/8 oz soft brown sugar
3 tbsp Horlicks
1 x 410 g can of evaporated
    milk
225 g/8 oz self-raising flour
1½ tsp bicarbonate of soda

For the icing
200 g/7 oz unsalted butter
340 g/12 oz plain chocolate
5½ tbsp Horlicks
85 g/3 oz icing sugar, sifted
3 tbsp milk
Maltesers for decoration

1. Preheat the oven to 170°C/ 325°F/Gas 3. Line two 12-hole muffin tins with paper cases.

2. Melt the butter and chocolate in a bowl over a pan of hot water, or chop the chocolate and place in a bowl in the microwave for 90 seconds.

3. When the chocolate is melted, beat in the eggs, one at a time, then the sugar. Stir the Horlicks into the evaporated milk and add half of it to the chocolate mixture. Sift the flour and bicarbonate and add half to the mixture. Then add the remaining milk and the rest of the flour.

4. Divide the mixture between the paper cases. Bake in the centre of the preheated oven for 20–25 minutes until springy to the touch. Remove and place the cakes on a wire rack to cool.

5. To make the icing, melt the butter and chocolate as before and stir in the Horlicks, sifted sugar and milk. Spoon the icing onto the cakes and decorate with Maltesers.

Lamingtons

y earliest cake memories are of these. There is something about the way the sponge is sodden with chocolate and the flakes of coconut cling to the sides that makes them completely irresistible. *Makes 30.*

225 g/8 oz unsalted butter, room temperature
340 g/12 oz caster sugar
2 tsp vanilla
4 eggs
340 g/12 oz self-raising flour
110 g/4 oz custard powder
240 ml/8 fl oz milk

For the icing
200 ml/7 fl oz milk
45 g/1½ oz butter
675 g/1 lb 8 oz icing sugar
55 g/2 oz cocoa powder
340 g/12 oz desiccated coconut

1. Preheat the oven to 170°C/325°F/Gas 3. Butter a baking sheet with raised edges, measuring about 25 x 50cm/10 x 20in, and sprinkle with flour.

2. Cream the butter, sugar and vanilla together until light and fluffy. Add the eggs, one at a time, beating each one in well. Sift the flour with the custard powder and add to the butter mixture, alternating with the milk.

3. Pour the mixture into the baking sheet and spread it evenly with a spatula. Bake in the centre of the oven for 35–40 minutes until springy to the touch. Remove from the oven and gently tip the slab of sponge onto a wire rack. Leave to cool completely, ideally overnight. Once the sponge is cool, cut it into 30 squares.

4. Now make the icing. Heat the milk and butter in a pan until the butter has melted. Sift the sugar and cocoa powder and add to the melted butter and milk. Remove from the heat and whisk to prevent any lumps forming. The consistency should be liquid but not too thin – the icing has to stick to the cakes and hold the coconut.

5. Put the desiccated coconut into a bowl. Using a skewer or a fork (or your fingers, my choice), dip the sponge cubes into the chocolate icing and once they are covered, roll them in the desiccated coconut. Place on a wire rack to set. Don't worry about getting a perfect finish – this is all about rustic charm. You will end up with chocolate in the coconut and sponge in the chocolate and the cubes won't be evenly covered but they will taste delicious.

Oatmeal toffee cookies

I remember these from my childhood. I would take great chewy bites while watching the colours of fireworks lighting up the night sky. The fact that they have oats in them makes it easy to convince yourself that eating them is an almost healthy experience. *Makes about 4 dozen.*

200 g/7 oz plain flour
1 tsp bicarbonate of soda
½ tsp salt
225 g/8 oz unsalted butter,
  room temperature
340 g/12 oz light brown sugar

2 large eggs, room temperature
2 tsp vanilla extract
285 g/10 oz oats
1 x 225 g/8 oz bag hard toffees,
  roughly chopped

1. Preheat the oven to 190°C/ 375°F/Gas 5. Line a baking sheet with baking parchment.

2. Sift together the flour, bicarbonate of soda and salt. Set aside.

3. Cream the butter and sugar until light and fluffy. Add the eggs, one at a time, beating well after each addition. Scrape down the sides of the bowl and mix in the vanilla.

4. Add the flour mixture to the butter, sugar and eggs and stir until the flour is just incorporated. Mix in the oats and toffee pieces.

5. Drop rounded teaspoons of dough onto the baking sheet, leaving about 5cm/2in between each one. Bake in the preheated oven for 8–10 minutes or until the edges are lightly browned. Remove and allow to cool for 2 minutes on the baking sheet, then transfer to a wire rack to cool.

Smartie cookies

These are much loved by adults and children alike. There is something delicious about the crunchiness of the Smarties' sugar coating contrasting with the chewy centre of the cookie. *Makes 24.*

225 g/8 oz unsalted butter,
room temperature
340 g/12 oz granulated sugar
85 g/3 oz soft dark brown
sugar

1 tsp vanilla extract
1 large egg and 1 egg yolk
425 g/15 oz self-raising flour
200 g/7 oz white chocolate
4 tubes of Smarties

1. Preheat the oven to 190°C/ 375°F/Gas 5. You will need a large ungreased baking sheet.

2. Cream the butter and sugars until light and fluffy, then add the vanilla, followed by the egg and yolk. Add the flour, a tablespoon at a time, and keep mixing until you have a soft dough.

3. Break the bar of chocolate into squares and cut each square in half to make about 50 pieces. Take a heaped tablespoon of the mixture and push in a couple of pieces of chocolate, making sure that the pieces are covered by the dough.

Place on the baking sheet, flatten with the palm of your hand and press in 5 or 6 Smarties. Repeat until all the dough and chocolate are used up, placing the cookies 5cm/2in apart on the baking sheet.

4. Bake in the preheated oven for about 10 minutes. Remove the cookies when they are just turning golden on top but before they look cooked through. They will continue to cook once removed from the oven. Leave them to cool on the baking sheet for 5–10 minutes until they are firm enough to transfer to a wire rack.

Butterscotch cookies

A s a small child, I would walk to the village shop on a Saturday with my older brother and sister to spend our hard-earned pocket money. They would buy sweets, but I would always buy a Caramac. Recently I realised that when American recipes call for butterscotch this is what they mean, so here is my version of butterscotch cookies. *Makes 20.*

110 g/4 oz plain flour, sifted
1 tsp bicarbonate of soda
½ tsp salt
55 g/2 oz unsalted butter,
   room temperature
110 g/4 oz granulated sugar

45 g/1½ oz dark brown sugar
1 tsp vanilla extract
1 egg, lightly beaten
2 Caramac bars, cut into pieces
55 g/2 oz chopped pecans

1. Preheat the oven to 190°C/ 375°F/Gas 5. You will need a large ungreased baking sheet.

2. Mix the flour, bicarbonate and salt together in a small bowl. Cream together the butter, sugars and vanilla in a large bowl and beat until creamy. Stir in the egg, followed by the flour mixture and mix all the ingredients together. Stir in the Caramac pieces and the nuts.

3. Drop rounded tablespoons of mixture onto the ungreased baking sheet. Bake for 10–12 minutes or until just golden on top. Remove from the tray and cool on a wire rack.

Chocolate chunk tray bake

This is a very easy version of chocolate chip cookies. It's an ideal recipe when you have lots of other things to do as you just tip the dough into the tray and cut into pieces when baked. Minimum fuss involved. *Makes 16.*

320 g/11 oz plain flour, unsifted
1 tsp bicarbonate of soda
1 tsp salt
110 g/4 oz unsalted butter, room temperature
170 g/6 oz granulated sugar

125 g/4½ oz soft brown sugar
1 tsp vanilla extract
2 eggs
340 g/12 oz chocolate chopped into 1cm/½in squares
110 g/4 oz chopped hazelnuts

1. Preheat the oven to 190°C/ 375°F/Gas 5. Grease a baking tin measuring about 38 x 25 x 2.5cm/ 15 x 10 x 1in.

2. Mix the flour, bicarbonate and salt together in a small bowl. Cream together the butter, sugars and vanilla in a large bowl and beat until creamy. Add the eggs, one at a time, and stir to combine. Then add in the flour mixture and mix well. Stir in the chocolate pieces and the nuts.

3. Spread the mixture evenly into the greased baking tin and bake for 20 minutes. Don't worry if it looks slightly underdone as it will continue to cook for a few minutes when it's out of the oven. Turn onto a wire rack to cool, then cut into 16 pieces.

Pecan puffs

oreish is a word that I am fond of using, but these take the term to a whole new level. It may be worth baking a double batch and hiding them away until the very last minute! *Makes 24.*

55 g/2 oz unsalted butter,
    room temperature
2 tbsp caster sugar
1 tsp vanilla essence

110 g/4 oz pecan nuts
110 g/4 oz self-raising flour
icing sugar

1. Preheat the oven to 180°C/350°F/Gas 4. You will need a large greased baking sheet.

2. Cream the butter and sugar together until pale and fluffy, and add the vanilla. Grind the nuts in a food processor or coffee grinder. Add the ground pecans and the flour to the creamed butter and stir well with a wooden spoon.

3. Roll heaped teaspoonfuls of dough into balls and place on the greased baking sheet. Bake for 30 minutes. Roll in icing sugar while still hot. To glaze, pop them back in the oven for 2 minutes. Remove and cool on a wire rack.

Index

This book has been a wonderfully collaborative project and there are so many people without whom it would never have happened: Sarah Lavelle, who stumbled across me and thought 'Cookie Girl' was a great idea for a book; I would like to thank her for standing by me. Photographer Simon Brown interpreted my vision with such great clarity and so little ego, helped brilliantly by stylist Tessa Evelegh, who never failed to astound me with her imaginative arrangements. Editor Jinny Johnson has shown huge patience with an inexperienced author. Designer Georgia has taken my 'fairytale' vision and created a palette of delicious and mouth-watering colours. Along the way I have been supported and encouraged by Mal Peachey at Essential Works and now Felicity Blunt and Jacquie Drewe at Curtis Brown. I thank them all for their wisdom and enthusiasm.

Nancy 'Noodle' Campbell is a shining star both in the kitchen and outside of it – I simply couldn't have done it without her. It was with her and my niece Sasha that I baked my first (of many) batches of cookies, little knowing then where it would lead me. Big thanks too to Saffron Goldup, Laura McNeur, Joanna Taylor, Caroline Robinson, Carlie Buckley, Victoria Cameron, Kelly Johnston, Steph Fairley, Waldo Wilkinson, Gabby Chelmicka, Gita Langley, Maria and Yvonne. For hair thanks to Michael at Unruly for Faye, Monica and Gracie; and for make-up, Debbie Walters' ladies. Nzame Richmond Shaw did a fantastic job, as did Caroline Simm. Thanks also to Sophie Harley for jewellery used in the book, and to Temperly and Iris for the dresses.

A great deal of credit must go to my dad, who has always been there to advise me, enthusiastically, on recipes. He set me on this path when he bought me my first baking book when I was five. My husband, who has been unwavering in his belief in me and tireless in his support, whether editing text or demolishing cakes. My two dear friends Daniel Norton and Ellie Tremain have been a huge help with the writing – I am eternally grateful to have such valuable opinions so close to hand. My daughter has been a great help, there is not a day goes by that she does not inspire me. My brother and sister, nieces and nephew, and all my friends have been tireless in their tasting and informative in their feedback, especially my big sis Sam, who may live on the other side of the world but is always here for me with her brilliant editing skills and creative writing experience. I would also like to express my gratitude to Helen and Cathy, the gorgeous girls at Green Row PR for their unwavering belief in my potential. Thanks too to Andy and Freddie at Jabberwokie for the website.

My biggest debt, however is to you out there reading this book, whether you know me from dropping by your office peddling my wares, or if you've read about my adventures elsewhere – you have created Cookie Girl and the journey I am on is thanks to every single one of you.

And finally my business partner Paul, for going beyond the call of duty in supporting me, believing in me and enabling me to finish this book – I am forever thankful.

An Aladdin's cave of baking essentials:

Kitchen Ideas
70 Westbourne Grove
London
W2 5SH
Tel: 020 7221 2777

Fabulous decorations online:

Cakes, Cookies and Crafts Shop
Morris Holbon Ltd
Unit 5 Woodgate Park
White Lund Industrial Estate
Morecambe
Lancashire
LA3 3PS
Tel: 05601 295610
www.cakescookiesandcraftsshop.co.uk

Decorations, colour paste and more:

Jane Asher Party Cakes and Sugarcraft
22–24 Cale Street
London
SW3 3QU
Tel: 020 7584 6177
www.jane-asher.co.uk

Not food-related, but for beautiful French furniture that we used in this book:

Sweetpea & Willow
3–5 St Johns Road
Isleworth
Middlesex
TW7 6NA
Tel: 0845 257 2627
www.sweetpeaandwillow.com

About the Author

Xanthe Milton is a writer and baker. She began selling her own home-made cookies and cakes when she took a break from acting – at first she delivered cookies on foot to offices in West London (figuring that people don't shut the door on warm cookies very often!), then set up a stall at Portobello Market. Later, her cupcakes were sold in Selfridges stores nationwide. She writes the 'Cookie Girl' column for The Grove magazine. Eat Me! is her first book. For more information visit www.cookiegirl.co.uk.